IFR PRINCIPLES AND PRACTICE

Self-Practice Exercises

for IFR Training and

Maintaining IFR Proficiency.

AVRAM GOLDSTEIN

PUBLISHED BY AIRGUIDE PUBLICATIONS
1207 Pine Ave., P.O. Box 1288, Long Beach, CA 90801

AVRAM GOLDSTEIN has spent his entire
career as a teacher. He is presently a professor at
Stanford University. He holds commercial and
instrument pilot ratings and is a certified flight
instructor and instrument flight instructor.

CONTENTS

(*Contents, continued*)

1. INTRODUCTION

Even if you rarely fly into clouds or carry out an approach under actual IFR conditions, the IFR rating will signify a degree of proficiency far exceeding what you've been satisfied with before. Your flying will be more confident and more relaxed, because you'll know how to fly the airplane precisely and automatically. You'll learn to hold 4000 feet, not 4050 sometimes and 3950 other times. You'll learn to hold a heading of 345°, not 337° sometimes and 353° other times. You'll learn to climb and descend and level off exactly, not approximately. You'll learn to make an approach at 80 knots, not 79 or 81. And you'll learn to communicate briskly, effectively, like a professional. These are the valuable byproducts of earning an IFR rating, but the main gains, of course, are in added safety and increased utility of your airplane. Low stratus that keeps the VFR pilot waiting to get off the ground will no longer delay you. And weather that turns marginal or worse will no longer spoil your trip and raise butterflies in your stomach.

If you already hold an IFR rating, you will be concerned with maintaining your proficiency, and you may even need some dual occasionally to meet the IFR currency requirements. This manual will therefore serve your needs too, even though it is written primarily for the aspiring candidate for a new IFR rating.

The IFR rating requires that you have 40 hours of actual or simulated (hood) time, but only 15 hours of this need be dual from a certificated instrument flight instructor (CIFI). To get the most out of your IFR instruction, you'll need to practice between sessions of dual instruction. And since you'll have to practice under the hood, you'll need another pilot with you in the right seat to watch for traffic and to keep you from flying into a hillside. How can you make these practice sessions most useful and productive? The same way a musician practices — by doing exercises, like scales, that are calculated to improve the different skills you have to learn, by constant application, evaluation, correction, and more practice. This manual is written for both of you — for you and for your check pilot. Before you fly, you should both study the exercise and know what you will be doing and how you will go about it. During the flight, your check pilot will read out instructions for you to follow or will invent instructions according to the plan outlined in each practice session. A scoring system will let you evaluate your progress as you repeat the maneuvers in each exercise.

Disorientation Exercises.

As you have undoubtedly read elsewhere, the most important thing in IFR flying is to trust the instruments, no matter what your senses tell you. This is hard to do. It requires practice and discipline. It is the key to survival in IFR conditions. Ask your instructor or check pilot to put you through some of the disorientation and vertigo maneuvers compiled by FAA. A few of the best ones are outlined below. They will help you to become convinced, through your own experience, that your normal senses are worthless in IFR conditions, and therefore have to be consciously suppressed as you give your full attention to the instruments. For these maneuvers you should close your eyes and lower your head. At the right moment you will be asked what you think the airplane is doing. Then open your eyes and see how wrong you are. A disorientation exercise serves its purpose when you are **absolutely convinced** the airplane is doing one thing when in fact, as you discover, it is doing something entirely different.

1. False sensation of climbing while turning. The ship is rolled very gradually and with good coordination into a 45° bank without change in altitude. The sensation produced is that of a climb, because of the increased G force.

2. False sensation of climbing while accelerating. From approach airspeed the ship is accelerated to cruise, maintaining straight-and-level attitude. The sensation produced is that of a climb.

3. False sensation of diving. A coordinated turn is entered as in #1 above, and then recovery to straight-and-level is initiated. You should be instructed to note your sensations and then open your eyes when recovery is about one-half completed. The sensation produced is that of diving, because of reduction of the G forces.

4. False sensation of tilting to right or left. The ship is put into a wings-level moderate skid. The sensation produced is that of tilting in the direction opposite to the skid.

5. False sensation of reversal of motion. The ship is rolled to a 45° banked attitude while holding the nose level and on a point with opposite rudder, as in a Dutch roll. Then the roll is abruptly stopped and held. The sensation produced is that of a strong sense of rotation to the opposite direction.

6. False sensation of diving or rolling beyond the vertical plane. The ship is started in a coordinated roll toward a 30° or 40° angle of bank. While this is in progress, bend your head and trunk down, look to the left or right (as though searching for some lost charts!), and resume the normal seated position with your eyes closed. The roll should be stopped just as you return to the upright position. Another version of this maneuver is to observe the entry into a steep descending gliding spiral, then lower your gaze to the floor. After about 20 seconds, bend your head and trunk down, look left or right as before, and resume the seated position with your eyes closed. In both these maneuvers the sensation produced is that of falling into the direction of the roll and downward. A severe degree of vertigo may ensue, which is dramatically instructive. As FAA says: "No explanation is needed in that the confusion speaks for itself."

Unusual Attitudes.

Disorientation exercises should be followed by practice in recovery from unusual attitudes, using only the turn indicator ("needle and ball") and airspeed indicator, i.e., with the attitude indicator (artificial horizon) covered. Unusual attitudes are typical of the results of vertigo, turbulence, and lapse of attention to the instruments, so they follow logically from the disorientation exercises. Unusual attitudes should only be practiced with an instructor, never with a check pilot who has no instructor rating. While the instructor places the airplane in an unusual attitude, often at the end of a disorientation maneuver, you will be under the hood with your head down and eyes closed. When the instructor says "You take it", you'll look at the panel, assess the situation, and immediately initiate the recovery. There are two categories of unusual attitude, which require different recovery techniques. They are distinguished by the behavior of the airspeed indicator.

(1) **Approach to a stall.** The airspeed is falling and you may also have the various cues to an approaching stall (wallowing, mushing, labored sound of the engine, etc.). The recovery procedure is identical to that for stall recoveries: simultaneously push the yoke forward and apply full power. Then, with the airplane flying again, level the wings with reference to the turn indicator, coordinating with rudder to center the ball. Once the incipient stall is eliminated, levelling the wings and bringing the airplane back to level flight is no problem.

(2) **Diving Spiral.** The airspeed is increasing, and you may also have the cue of a racing engine. Here you must reduce the power to idle immediately, then level the wings. Finally, you can pull gently out of the dive with back pressure on the yoke. If you pull back on the yoke before the wings are level you may well only tighten the spiral, or even enter a stall or spin.

For the sake of consistency this manual is written with the typical light trainer in mind, specifically the Piper Cherokee series, but it is equally applicable with small modifications to the Cessna line or to other airplanes. The various exercises will have to be adapted to meet local conditions — the local terrain, traffic density, and availability of different kinds of navaids. Wherever the terms "he" or "him" are used in referring to pilots, check pilots, instructors, or FAA examiners, they should be understood to mean "he or she" or "him or her"; saving space and avoiding clumsy sentences should not be misunderstood as sexist bias.

Finally, the limitations of this manual should be understood. It is not a substitute for a good instructor; there is no substitute. Nor is it a substitute for thorough manuals and handbooks about instrument flying. Of these there are many. Especially recommended are the FAA's own **Instrument Flying Handbook** and two simpler and very well organized books: **Instrument Pilot's Guide** by L. Reithmaier (Aero Publishers, Inc., Fallbrook, Calif. 92028), and **Instrument Flight Manual** by W. K. Kershner (Iowa State University Press, Ames, Iowa). In a class by itself for superbly clear explanation of ATC procedures is **Instruments: Procedures and Techniques** by T. F. McMahon (Flite Training Aids, Federal Way, Washington 98002).

Despite every effort, errors (typographic and otherwise) are bound.to creep into any publication. I welcome corrections and criticisms from readers in the hope of improving future editions. To my own instructors over the years — Patricia Gladney, Pat Daily, and John Ludwig — who led me from joy to joy in the art of flying, I express my gratitude and appreciation. I am grateful to Leslie Parrish for her helpful comments on the manuscript, to Cheryl LoMaglio for expert secretarial assistance, and to Faith Hornbacher for the art work.

2. PRE-TAKEOFF PROCEDURES

Principles.

Flight Log. The secret of safe smooth IFR flight is systematic organization in the cockpit. You'll become expert in handling the airplane, of course, but if things are disorganized, if you can't find things when you need them, you'll surely come to grief sooner or later. Your flight bag should have a specific place for every item you may need, and you should be able to reach for that item and find it without more than a glance. Seemingly trivial things become important in tight situations. What happens when you break the lead in your pencil? Do you carry some spares, and do you know where to find them? What about a flashlight? It could be a life saver if you're unexpectedly delayed until after dark, and your panel lighting fails. Can you lay hands on each part of the Airman's Information Manual, without scrambling through a lot of maps and papers? You may need it to look up some characteristics of the airport you're making an unplanned approach to. Is your computer within easy reach? Are your Enroute charts and approach charts properly organized in a binder, and have you kept them up to date? Until you develop the technique of systematic organization, you can not be a fully proficient IFR pilot.

An important part of organizing your flight is the keeping of a good flight log. There are many possibilities for doing this. Figs. 2-1a and 2-1b show the *Airguide Flight Log*, available in pads from Airguide Publications, 1207 Pine Avenue, P.O. Box 1288, Long Beach, California 90813. Let's go through it step by step, and discuss the importance of various items.

At top right you can record the date. On the first line you enter the departure point and the total nautical miles for the flight. In the first four columns at left you enter your entire route, fix by fix, with magnetic course, route (airway), and VOR frequency for each leg. On each line enter, in the ninth column, under "Miles Betwn Fix", the nautical miles to be flown, as read off the enroute chart. Compute and enter, in the last column, the total miles remaining to destination. Then, using your estimated ground speed, compute and enter, in the sixth column, under "Est. Mins. to Fix", the estimated time for that leg. Add up all entries in this column, to obtain total time for the flight, and enter it at upper right, under the date.

AIRGUIDE PUBLICATIONS
1207 PINE AVE., P.O. Box 1288
LONG BEACH, CA 90801

ENROUTE FLIGHT LOG

DATE

TOTAL TIME

Fixes	Mag. Course	Route	Freq.	ESTIMATED		ACTUAL		Miles Betwn Fix	Ground Speed	Total Miles Remain
				ETA Next Fix	Est. Mins.to Fix	Time Over Fix	Elaps- ed Time			
LGB	← DEPARTURE POINT					TOTAL MILES →				321
SLI	100	DIR	115.7	T.O. &	Climb	0755	10	5	↗	316
ONT	058	V8	112.2	0805	0+10	0804	9	27	160	289
PMS	078	V16	115.5	0826	0+22			59		230
BLH	085		117.4					85		145
BXK	080		110.6					98		47
PHX	077	↓	115.6					47		0

POSITION REPORT:	ACFT. IDENT.	POSITION	TIME	ALT.	IFR/VFR	EST. NEXT FIX	NAME OF SUCCEEDING FIX	PIREPS

CLEARANCE

FLIGHT TIME	Tach. Out-		Tach. In-		FUEL REQUIRED		VFR CRUISE ALTS.
Station	Take Off	Land	Total Time		To Dest.		3000 ft. above ground

FUEL REQUIRED

VFR CRUISE ALTS.
3000 ft. above ground
360° - 179°, Odd + 500'
ALL COURSES MAGNETIC
180° - 359°, Even + 500'

Station	Take Off	Land	Total Time
LGB	0745	✕	✕
PHX		0940	1+55

FUEL REQUIRED	
To Dest.	
To Alternate	
App. + Reserve	
Total Reqrd.	
Total Aboard	
Extra	

CALL   XMIT   REC.

TIME SWITCH TANKS			
1		3	
2		4	

RADIO 122.2 122.2
(Primary universal frequency)
RADIO 122.1 **VOR**
RADIO 123.6 123.6
(Airport advisory)
RADIO 122.0 122.0
(Weather channel)
UNICOM 122.8 122.8
Arpt w/Tower123.0 123.0
Plane to Plane122.9 122.9

Fig. 2-1a

AIRGUIDE PUBLICATIONS
1207 PINE AVENUE
LONG BEACH, CALIFORNIA 90813

WEATHER LOG
Date-

WINDS ALOFT

Station	3000 Deg/Vel	6000 Deg/Vel	9000 Deg/Vel	12,000 Deg/Vel	18,000 Deg/Vel	24,000 Deg/Vel	30,000 Deg/Vel

CURRENT WEATHER

Station	Ceiling & Sky	Vsby Lity	Weather	Tmp.	Dew Pt.	Wind Dir./Vel.	Alt. Set.

FORECAST WEATHER

Station	Terminal & Alternate Forecast Weather - ETE Plus 2 Hours.

FLIGHT PLAN FORM

1. Flight plan: IFR VFR DVFR	2. Plane No.	3. Plane type: Transponder DME.
4. Est. TAS K	5. Depart. pt.	6. Dept. time	7. Cruising Altitude

8. Route of flight

9. Destination	10. Est. time enroute: Hrs. Mins.	11. Remarks
12. Fuel: Hrs. Mins.	13. Alt.	14. Pilot	Ph:
15. No. people	16. Color	Address	Home Base

Fig. 2-1b

You will have had a weather briefing, and this should be recorded on the back side (Fig. 2-1b), under "FORECAST WEATHER", together with winds aloft forecasts, under "WINDS ALOFT" at top of page. From the winds aloft you will have computed your estimated ground speed, and this will have been used to obtain your estimated minutes for each leg.

The moment you are cleared onto the runway for takeoff, you should enter the **actual time** and the **tachometer reading** opposite "FLIGHT TIME" on the front side of the form. This is a critical entry, for your **fuel-exhausted time** can only be computed with reference to it. Since you know your total time enroute estimate, you can add that to your departure time to get an ETA at your destination, and this too should be recorded.

Before takeoff you should have set your altimeter. Put the setting in the window, then check the needles against field elevation. If the discrepancy exceeds 75 feet, the altimeter is outside the permissible limits of accuracy and should not be depended upon. Why not set the altimeter to field elevation, note the discrepancy in the setting window, then add or subtract that amount whenever you are given a new altimeter setting? Because altimeter error may not be the same at all altitudes, so you could end up inaccurate by much more than the allowable 75 feet. But there is a common-sense exception. If you are going to make IFR approaches nearby, and your altimeter shows too high at the start, you should certainly correct it, or you will be lower than you think on the approach.

As you fly along, you enter your estimated time of arrival (ETA) for the next fix (usually a VOR), line by line as the flight progresses. As you reach a fix, enter the actual time over fix, and compute the actual elapsed time from the previous fix. By dividing the "Miles Betwn Fix" by the "Elapsed Time", you obtain your actual ground speed, which should be entered in the tenth column. Now this actual ground speed is applied to the next leg to obtain your ETA at the fix. Thus, leg by leg, you'll be able to see if you're running on plan, or slow, or fast. And at any point, by dividing "Total Miles Remain" by the actual ground speed, you can revise your ETA at destination.

Before you start, include the segment of the flight from your destination to your alternate. If you have to use your alternate at all, it will be because the weather is below minimums at your destination. After a couple of missed approaches, you'll be in poor condition to start computations on getting to the alternate. Have it all down in advance!

The position report format is given on the flight log for your convenience, although in today's radar environment such reports have become rare.

Moving down Fig. 2-1a, the next area is for recording clearances as you receive them during the course of the flight. A good common-sense shorthand is valuable here. Assigned headings and altitudes should be recorded as they are received, expecially during radar vectoring. It is amazing how you can forget the heading. You turn toward the new heading well enough when it is assigned, but then you become distracted. When you look at the heading indicator (directional gyro, DG) again, it says 155. Was that the assignment? Or was it 145 or 165? Or you're cleared to descend to 7000 and report level. You start the descent just fine, but again, a little distraction, you look back at the altimeter and it is just passing through 6700. Were you supposed to level at 7000? Or was that what the controller said to someone else on the frequency? Being able to refer to a written notation is a real comfort.

What about frequency assignments? With two radios, the best procedure is to alternate, first one, then the other, so the previous frequency is always still set up. But with a single radio, keeping a written record of every frequency is absolutely essential. Record each new frequency assigned, at the time it is assigned, and **before you switch.** It very often happens that you switch to the assigned frequency and find you can't make contact. Maybe the new transmitter is out of range because of your altitude, maybe the new transmitter is inoperative or too garbled to read, maybe your receiver is defective on that frequency, maybe your transmitter doesn't work on that frequency. You are in real trouble if you can't return at once to the controller you've been talking to, and tell him "Negative contact on 120.1 (or whatever)". The FSS frequencies listed at the bottom right are convenient reminders, should you wish to leave the ATC frequency (get permission first!) to get weather or airport information from a flight service station.

At bottom center is a little table for recording your fuel management if you don't have a crossfeeding system. Don't depend on fuel gauges; they can fail at the most critical times. You should know exactly how much fuel you started with. Then the time record tells you how much fuel remains in each tank, since you know the fuel consumption of your aircraft at cruise power.

On the back side (Fig. 2-1b) is an area for recording actual weather at stations enroute. At the bottom is the basic format for filing an IFR flight plan. It is convenient to have it right here, especially for "pop-up" filing, should a VFR flight run into IFR weather enroute.

Checklist. An IFR checklist serves the same purpose as the VFR checklists you are used to, but it is far more important. The safety of an IFR flight depends upon all systems operating porperly. Once you're on your way it is no time to discover that your gyro instruments are inoperative, that your altimeter is broken, or that your NAV or COM receivers don't work. In VFR flight such problems will cause inconvenience; in IFR flight they may produce a critical emergency.

Surprisingly, even experienced pilots may never have developed really adequate checklist discipline. One purpose of the checklist is to ensure that every single item is covered before you take off. Since you will certainly be interrupted from time to time before takeoff, it is absolutely essential that the checklist items be numbered sequentially, and that the sequence be followed faithfully every time. Then whenever you are interrupted, you have only to note the number of the item you are working on, and pick it up again there when you resume checking. It is very instructive to read CAB accident reports on commercial airline accidents in which interruption of a checklist resulted in skipping an important item, which, in turn became the cause of a crash. If it can happen to ATR pilots with thousands of hours — familiarity breeds contempt! — it can happen to you. So develop a sound procedure that you never vary.

The second purpose of a checklist is to provide an appropriate time when each particular instrument or operational system can be put through its paces. A good example is checking the fuel pump in a low-wing aircraft. Normally, fuel pressure is maintained by the engine driven fuel pump. The electric pump is a backup. Notice that once the engine is operating, there is no possible way to check the operation of the electric pump, since fuel pressure will be adequate whether it is on or off. Therefore, the electric fuel pump is turned on very early in the checklist, before the engine is started, and the fuel pressure gauge is monitored to be sure the pump is working. Now notice the second point: With the electric pump on, there is no possible way to verify that the engine driven pump is operating. Therefore, once the engine is running, you turn off the electric pump and taxi without it. Finally, before takeoff, knowing that both pumps are really working, you turn on the electric pump again.

Similar safeguards are employed to check all your redundant systems. Call ground control on one radio, switch to tower on the second radio. Then you know that both are working.

The only time you can find out if your turn indicators are working before you take off and they become absolutely critical is during taxi. There are three instruments that should show a turn during taxi — first a right turn, then a left turn — and you should check them all: your turn needle or turn coordinator, your DG, and your magnetic compass.

The only time you will know if your brakes work before you'll need them on a landing roll is during taxi; try them out and make sure.

The checking of the instrument panel is one continuous operation, the details of which will depend upon the way your panel is laid out, and it will usually be different for each aircraft. The important thing is to start at one point, say the upper left, and systematically check each instrument one by one, moving across to the right, then back to the left on the second row, over to the right again, then down to the row of engine instruments, switches, and so on, including fuses and circuit breakers and whatever else is there. A pilot who does this systematically and confidently will complete the job more quickly as well as more thoroughly than one who skips around in a haphazard fashion, or even skips over instruments along the way. An instructor or FAA examiner can tell a lot about how a checkride will go in those few minutes at the runup area, just watching the way the instrument panel is checked. I have seen IFR students — for no reason I or they could explain — start at the left, jump right past the clock (for example) and start checking the artificial horizon. But the clock is important. Suppose it quit because it wasn't wound; the typical place that would happen would be about 2 minutes after leaving a final approach fix inbound on a nonprecision approach. As a matter of fact, the clock should have been set when you first called for taxi clearance: "San Jose ground control, Cherokee 2345 Juliet at tie-down Oscar 20, IFR Sacramento, time check." Telling him right at the start that you're IFR and where you're going alerts him to phone Center and get your clearance for you. Asking for a time check at this point tells him you're a pro — or trying to behave like one — and reassures him that you know what you're doing. The other way — later on in the middle of your checklist asking: "Oh by the way would you mind giving me a time check" — is sloppy, and it also clutters up the frequency unnecessarily.

The reason my checklist says simply "Entire Instrument Panel", rather than specifying Clock, DG, AI, and so on, is that **everything** on the instrument panel has to be checked, without exception. The instrument panel "checklist" is all there in front of you; use a forefinger and **touch** the instruments, switches, dials, fuses, circuit breakers, and whatever, one by one, and adjust whatever needs adjusting. When your finger touches the DG, set it. When you touch the AI, position the little airplane on the artificial horizon. When you touch the VSI, see if it really reads zero, as it should. When you touch the VOR, set and check it, as described below. When you touch the pitot heat, turn it on and see if your ammeter shows the heavy drain it should. When you have completed an instrument panel check like this, you'll **know** that everything is in working order, and you'll be ready to fly. This system has the great advantage that in an unfamiliar ship you'll be obliged to become acquainted with each and every instrument and switch before you fly, despite the fact that different panels are laid out in different ways.

At the least convenient moment, either while you are taxiing or in the middle of your pre-takeoff checklist, ground control will call you with your clearance. The peremptory way it suddenly blasts into what you're doing — "45 Juliet CLEARANCE" — makes you want to drop everything and pick up your pencil. Don't do it. You are only being told that clearance is ready when you want it — when **you** want it. The cool reply is: "45 Juliet, stand by''. Then go about your business and when you **are** ready, call: "45 Juliet, ready to copy''. Even better — until you are very experienced — say: "45 Juliet, ready to copy, and would you mind reading it slowly, please.''. Actually, it will be a lot faster than having to ask for numerous repeats, and the ground controller will therefore appreciate it too. After copying the clearance, you will again have a tendency to rush things by reading it back at once. Again, don't do it. Same answer as before: "45 Juliet, stand by''. Now study the clearance, and be sure you understand it and are able to comply with it. You might not be able to climb fast enough to reach some specified crossing altitude in time. You might not have a DME aboard when that's the only way to identify CALABASH intersection. If you read back a clearance, you've signed a contract to comply. When you're ready, then, read it back — or ask for changes if necessary. There's still no hurry. Go on with your checklist if it's not complete, get everything set in the cockpit, tune the needed COM and NAV frequencies in advance (when you switch to tower on #2 radio, change #1 from ground control to departure control). Then call tower: "45 Juliet ready to go, IFR Sacramento''. The usual response will now be: "45 Juliet, hold for departure release.'' At this point the tower controller calls departure control on the phone and tells him you're ready to go. As soon as you can be worked into the IFR traffic, you'll be cleared for takeoff.

A few words are in order about checking your VOR, DME, and ADF receivers. If you have dual VOR and you can receive any VOR station at the runup position on your airport, you can make a legal VOR check and enter it in the aircraft logbook kept for the purpose. Regulations require that two VOR indicators checked against each other must agree within 4 degrees, so center both needles exactly, and enter into your log the exact OBS readings of both. If they disagree by more than 4 degrees, you'll have to fly (VFR) to an officially designated ground or air VOR checkpoint and find out which one is malfunctioning, or use a designated VOT (test station) for the same purpose.

Every aircraft will require its own unique checklist. You should construct one to fit your own ship, and modify it through experience until it's perfect. The printed checklists furnished by airplane manufacturers are wholly inadequate, as are the abbreviated ones placarded on your instrument panel. Fig. 2-2 presents my own IFR checklist for my Cherokee 180, presented only as an example of what a complete checklist for a particular ship should be like.

A certain few checklist items belong in a special category called PRE-TAKEOFF, at the very end of the runup. There are good reasons. "Doors and Windows'' is an example. In uncomfortably hot weather, expecially if you have passengers, you will without doubt keep the doors and windows open as long as possible. Thus, to be sure they are secure before takeoff, this item has to be checked just before you roll onto the runway, not sooner. "Flaps" and "Trim" are in the same category for another reason. If you are practicing in the pattern, you will not return to the runup area after your first landing; you'll just taxi back and be ready to go again. This gives you a splendid chance to take off with heavy nose-up trim, full flaps, and door open. To ensure that such essential items are checked before every takeoff, I use a simple memory aid that I repeat **every time I roll onto a runway**: FOR TAKEOFF DO THIS CHECK. The first letters of the five words stand for the important items. F stands for FLAPS/FUELPUMP. T stands for TRIM. D stands for DOORS—WINDOWS. T stands for TRANSPONDER. C stands for CARB HEAT—COWL FLAPS.

Practice.

For pre-takeoff procedures there are no varied sample exercises of the kind that will be presented in all the subsequent chapters. The only requirement here is to follow the checklist accurately and in a professional manner. The role of the check pilot is to act as an instructor would — to monitor the whole procedure and to evaluate the competence with which it is carried out. The check pilot should have a copy of the checklist and should follow it step by step. Score 10 points for each item skipped. During the complete check of the instrument panel, score 10 points for each instrument, gauge, or switch not physically touched and correctly adjusted. The check pilot should also interrupt from time to time on one pretext or another, in a deliberate attempt to simulate interruptions that might normally occur. For example, in the middle of the instrument panel check a distracting conversation might be started concerning a supposed malfunction of a seat belt or a seat adjustment, or attention might be drawn to another aircraft on the ramp. It is also legitimate for the check pilot to "forget" to fasten his seat belt (it is the pilot's responsibility to ensure that all passengers are securely fastened in), or to close a door without properly latching it. These are the ways a FAA examiner may eventually test the applicant's competence in a check ride, and it is good practice for the pilot to get used to them.

An important type of practice the check pilot can give is to invent clearances for the pilot to copy. Here again, taking the role of the controller in the tower, the check pilot should unexpectedly interrupt during taxiing or during the runup with: "2345 Juliet clearance". Score 10 points if the pilot permits this to take precedence over his more important tasks of the moment. When, at the right time, the pilot announces: "45 Juliet ready to copy", the check pilot should read out a clearance. Only the limits of creative imagination restrict these "clearances", which should become longer and more complicated with increasing practice. An example of a simple clearance might be: "2345 Juliet is cleared to the Reno airport as filed, maintain 9000 (niner thousand), departure control is 121.3, squawk 4325 on departure." A more complicated clearance might be: "2345 Juliet is cleared to the Reno airport via radar vectors to Sunol intersection, Victor 244 South to Stockton,

IFR CHEROKEE 180 CHECKLIST

PREFLIGHT
1. Fuel Selector: ON
2. Yoke: FREE
3. Flaps: 40°
4. Walkaround: DRAIN SUMPS, OIL OVER 6

5. Flaps: RETRACT
6. Flight log/tach: CHECK
7. Brake: SET
8. Switches: AVIONICS AND PANEL ALL OFF
9. Mixture: RICH
10. Prime: IF NEEDED
11. Throttle: CRACKED
12. Master: ON
13. Fuel Pump: ON, CHECK PRESSURE, OFF
14. "CLEAR"
15. Mags: BOTH, PUSH TO START
16. Throttle: IDLE AT 1200 RPM
17. Oil Pressure: CHECK
18. Radios: ON
19. Transponder: STANDBY
20. Information: RUNWAY, WIND, ALTIMETER, TIME

TAXI
21. Brakes: CHECK
22. Left/Right Turns: CHECK TURN INDICATOR,
        DG, MAGNETIC COMPASS

RUNUP AREA
23. Brake: SET
24. Entire Instrument Panel, left to right, top
        to bottom: CHECK AND SET, including VOR's
        legal IFR, circuit breakers.
25. Runup: 2000 RPM
        MAGS (175 max drop, 50 difference)
        SUCTION 5 INCHES
        CARB HEAT
        FULL IDLE, THEN 1200 RPM
26. Carb Heat: IF NEEDED
27. Controls: FREE
28. Seats and Belts: CHECK

Fig. 2-2

Continued on next page . . .

PRE-TAKEOFF (Whenever taxiing onto runway)
29. For = F = FLAPS/FUEL PUMP
30. Takeoff = T = TRIM
31. Do = D = DOORS-WINDOWS
32. This = T = TRANSPONDER CODE AND ON
33. Check = C = CARB HEAT OFF/COWL FLAPS OPEN

LEAVING PATTERN
F = FLAPS RETRACTED
F = FUEL PUMP OFF
T = TIME: RECORD

LEVELLING FOR CRUISE
F = FUEL SELECTOR: Change Tanks
M = MIXTURE: Lean as required

PA 28-180 NUMBERS
Best rate climb = 85 MPH (74 KNOTS)
Best angle climb = 74 MPH (64 KNOTS)
Enroute climb = 100 MPH (87 KNOTS)
Best glide angle = 80 MPH (70 KNOTS)
Final approach = 80 MPH (70 KNOTS)
IFR approach = 92 MPH (80 KNOTS)
Stall, wings level, no flaps = 68 MPH (59 KNOTS)
Stall, wings, level, 40° flaps = 61 MPH (53 KNOTS)

SHUTDOWN
1. Throttle: FULL IDLE
2. Switches: AVIONICS + PANEL OFF EXCEPT MASTER
3. Mixture: LEAN CUTOFF
4. Master: OFF
5. Mags: OFF AND REMOVE KEY
6. Flight log/tach: RECORD
7. Instrument panel: COVER
8. Yoke: LASH WITH SEATBELT
9. Door: LOCK AND LATCH
10. Baggage compartment: CHECK LOCKED
11. Tiedown: COMPLETE
12. Flight Plan: CLOSE IF NOT ALREADY CLOSED

Fig. 2-2 Continued

Continued on next page . . .

IFR APPROACH
Before Final Approach Fix
1. ATIS, ALTIMETER SET, DG SET
2. SET, IDENTIFY, TEST:
    —COMs/NAVs/Marker Beacons/ADF/DME
3. REVIEW APPROACH AND MISSED APPROACH
At Final Approach Fix

1. ALTITUDE CHECK
2. LANDING CHECKLIST ON PANEL
3. SLOW TO IFR APPROACH SPEED (80 KNOTS)
4. START INBOUND TIMING
5. REPORT AS INSTRUCTED

Fig. 2-2 Continued

End.

flight plan route. Turn right on departure heading 060 for radar vectors to Sunol. Maintain 3000, expect 7000 at Sunol. Report passing 2000. Departure control 121.3, squawk 1143.'' Ideally, these invented clearances should correspond to actual routes on the enroute charts, so that the pilot can check and verify them before reading back. Then the readback is checked for accuracy. There is no penalty for requesting repetition (''Say again''), but score 10 points for every error in readback, and 20 points for accepting a clearance with which it is impossible to comply. To make matters more difficult, when the pilot has reached a good level of proficiency with ordinary clearances, the check pilot should deliberately introduce clearances that are in error or cannot be complied with. For example, ''cross Sunol at 7000'' when that would require an impossible rate of climb, or including an ADF intersection when the aircraft has no ADF equipment, or including a DME fix when there is no DME aboard, or even including an altitude well below the MOCA (minimal obstacle clearance altitude). The purpose of all this is to train the pilot to question and doublecheck every clearance, for the safety of the flight takes precedence over everything else.

Finally, the check pilot should pace his rate of delivery to the increasing proficiency of the pilot, so that experience is gained in copying accurately faster and faster clearances.

Keeping a record of the score at each practice session should provide a visual indication of progress. The last item on the score sheet asks the check pilot to make a subjective evaluation of the smoothness and efficiency of the pilot's performance. This includes also whether or not the tasks are accomplished with reasonable speed. Score 20 points for a bumbling, outrageously slow performance; 10 points for moderate floundering and uncertainty; zero for snappy professionalism. The ultimate aim, of course, is zero score in all categories.

Score Sheet

Session:	1	2	3	4	5	6	7	8	9	10
Date:										
ITEM Disorganized cockpit or procedures (20 points each).										
Checklist items skipped (10 points each)										
Instruments, switches, etc. skipped or not adjusted properly. (10 points each)										
Errors caused by distractions (10 points each)										
Clearance readback errors. (10 points each)										
Accepting impossible clearance. (20 points each)										
Incorrect or omitted settings of NAV and COM in advance of takeoff. (10 points each)										
TOTAL POINT SCORE										

3. IFR COMMUNICATIONS

Principles.

The 10 Commandments of ATC. Students embarking on a course of IFR instruction are usually terrified of the strange rapid-fire instructions from the controller, which seem unintelligible or barely intelligible, yet have to be understood and complied with. All instructions (clearances) from ATC should be repeated back, routinely and snappily, to verify that you heard them and wrote them down correctly. In the clouds, you certainly would not want to turn to a heading of two-five-zero when the controller said three-five-zero; sooner or later a mistake like that could be fatal. To get into the habit of repeating back, whenever your instructor plays the role of ATC controller, or in these practice exercises when your pilot friend in the right seat reads out a clearance, always repeat it back, then carry it out.

Much of the fear about copying clearances, whether they are short ("Turn right to 220 degrees") or long ("2345 Juliet cleared to Shark intersection via Victor 44, cross Shrimp at or above 3000 . . . etc.") comes from uncertainty as to what strange things might suddenly be thrown at you. By learning through practice what you can expect the controller to say at each point in your IFR flight, you can become more proficient at understanding him when he does say it. A great help in this regard is to listen to the ATC frequencies at home, without the distractions of flying the airplane. The cost of an aircraft-band VHF receiver is a good investment, and you can while away many profitable hours learning the patter and what it means. You will find, then, that nearly everything ATC has to say boils down to 10 kinds of instruction, which I call "the 10 commandments of ATC". Here they are, and what you do about them.

1. **Climb (descend) and maintain _____.**
   Example: ATC: "2345 Juliet, climb and maintain 5000."
   You: "45 Juliet climb and maintain 5000. And we're leaving 3000 for 5000."

The first part is just your acknowledgement that you heard what the controller said. The last bit is required because leaving an assigned altitude is a compulsory report to ATC. If you want to be very professional, you can even say "Leaving 3 for 5", as you will hear the 747 and DC-10 captains do.

It's faster, and in this business, snappier communications are the aim, so as not to clutter the frequency. The controller may be busy with a lot of people besides you.

Although not compulsory, it's a very good idea always to report reaching an assigned altitude. It reminds him that you're there, and what altitude you're at, and it let's you hear a comforting "Roger" in return. This is especially nice when you're the only one he's handling, and you wonder if your receiver has gone dead. The report would be "45 Juliet level at 5".

Once you're in communication with the controller and staying on the same frequency, never call him by name again. The first time, you said "Oakland Center, 2345 Juliet level at 3 (or whatever)". On subsequent calls, just say your message. **You** know you're talking to Oakland Center, and **he** knows you're on the frequency. Therefore, as above, just push the mike button, say "45 Juliet level at 5", and release it. It takes 3 seconds, his "Roger 45 Juliet" takes 2, and that's that.

2. Turn right (left) heading _____.
   Example: ATC: "45 Juliet turn left heading 180."
        You: "45 Juliet left to 180." And do it.

Controllers are human. Sometimes they'll say left when they mean right. If your heading is 150 and he says "left to 180", does he **really** want you to make a left turn for nearly a full circle? Question it: "45 Juliet, our heading is 150, do you want LEFT to 180?" ATC: "Negative, RIGHT to 180."

The whole trick is to know what's going on and to know where you are at all times. On rare occasions a controller has tragically misidentified a plane and flown it into a mountainside. If you're being vectored toward a mountainside (know the terrain, use the sectional chart as well as the instrument chart), don't hesitate to ask about it. Reticence could make you a rare but nonetheless real statistic. Coming into Albuquerque once in heavy IFR weather from the East I was vectored down to 10,000 feet and told "02 Foxtrot turn right heading 330." Sandia Mountain (10,877 MSL), it seemed to me, would be straight ahead. I: "This is 02 Foxtrot. Do you really mean 330 at my altitude?" ATC: "02 Foxtrot **immediate** left turn to 220". Did he say it wrong, or did I hear it wrong? It doesn't matter. It pays to question.

3. Immediate right (left) turn . . . Stop turn.

This command is complied with instantly. **Immediate** means do it right now and there's a reason for it, you can bet. Roll into the turn, **then** acknowledge. The non-emergency circumstance for this command is during a precision radar approach with gyros out. Then, since you have no way of turning accurately to headings, all the turn commands are given this way.

4. Say altitude. Do it. "45 Juliet descending through three thousand four hundred."

5. Say heading. Do it. "45 Juliet heading 165."

6. Cleared . . .

This is the one that can get complicated. Pencil and paper helps. It may be simple: "45 Juliet cleared for the approach." Or it could be a complete change in your routing, full of airways and intersections you never heard of, holding instructions, expect further clearance time, and what-not. The proper answer to this command, in the air as on the ground, unless you fully understand and can comply, is simply: "45 Juliet stand by." Then work it out, and when you're ready, call and read it back. Remember, to acknowledge a clearance is to accept it. If you can't comply (e.g., don't have the right navigational equipment, or can't increase speed sufficiently), or you don't like it (e.g., it takes your single-engine bird 10 miles out to sea), tell the controller so, and negotiate a better clearance. Usually you'll get courteous cooperation.

7. Squawk _____.

Here a transponder code will be given, such as "45 Juliet squawk 0145". This command and the next one should not be acknowledged. Just do it. The reason is clear if you understand what is going on. The controller you've been with is usually preparing to hand you off to the next sector, which may be controlled by the man or woman sitting right next to him (in which case he leans over, points out your radar return, and says "That's 2345 Juliet at 5000 I'm handing him over"), or by a controller somewhere else (in which case the transaction is carried out by telephone). In any case, when you squawk the new code it will be obvious on the new controller's radar, which is selectively tuned to that code. If they don't see you squawking the right code, you'll hear about it. During cruise at moderate altitudes, you will pass from sector to sector of one ATC center, and eventually to another center, without changing code. But approach and departure controllers may use special codes to distinguish their low-altitude traffic from high-altitude traffic cruising above their airspace. And increasingly, discrete codes are being assigned, using the last two digits to give each airplane its own code. Thus, you may get codes like 0145 or 1106. Discrete codes are used especially with automatic altitude reporting transponders, so that each aircraft's altitude is displayed next to its "blip" on the controller's radar screen.

8. Ident.

Again, don't acknowledge. Just touch the IDENT button on your transponder. This will produce a bright double slash on your radar return, to identify you unmistakeably. This command is used in many handoffs, to confirm for the new controller that your blip is indeed 2345 Juliet. It also may be used any time there is the slightest uncertainty in the controller's mind as to who is who in his airspace. When you IDENT **for the first time only**, you will hear "2345 Juliet radar contact 2 miles southeast of Saratoga (or wherever)". But for the rest of your flight you'll probably never hear that again. When the new controller says "2345 Juliet IDENT", and you do, and he confirms that you are you, he won't tell you about it. So don't worry. And never under any circumstances touch the IDENT button without being told to or (if you wanted to test your transponder) getting permission first. Otherwise you risk causing a misidentification with some other airplane that may have been asked to IDENT. Misidentification can be unhealthy when you're IFR under radar control.

9. Contact (facility) on (frequency).
> Example. ATC: "2345 Juliet contact Los Angeles Center on 125.65."
> You: "45 Juliet to 125.65. Thank you and good day."
> ATC: "Have a good flight."

Don't indulge in the courtesies if the controller is terribly busy; it wastes his time and he has a lot to do. But otherwise, it's good practice. A pleasant level of politeness at all times pays off. The ATC controller has a high-pressure high-tension worrisome job with fearful responsibilities. Keeping things calm, cool, and pleasant under all circumstances is the best way to continue getting the efficient service you need. Snarling, sarcasm, or irritability only provoke resentment and hostility, qualities that don't help anyone, least of all you, who are utterly dependent on his doing his job correctly. The little amenities, when there's time for them, tell the controller that you appreciate his efforts and know how tough his job is; and he is telling you that he knows it's not easy bouncing around in turbulence, trying to hold altitude, and flying where you're supposed to.

The command to change frequency means a handoff. It follows logically the previous step of preparing for the handoff, which may have involved a change in transponder code. So you know what's coming next when you get a code change.

> ATC: "2345 Juliet squawk 0200."
> You: Do it. Then there will be a pause of a minute or so.
> ATC: "45 Juliet contact Los Angeles Approach Control 121.3."
> You: "45 Juliet to 121.3, good evening, sir."
> You: Switch frequency to 121.3 **then listen**. When it's quiet, call: "2345 Juliet with you at 3000."
> ATC (now the Approach Controller): "2345 Juliet IDENT."

You: Do it.

ATC: Silence. Everything is fine. The handoff is complete.

10. Traffic _____ o'clock, _____ miles, slow (fast).

If ATC knows what the traffic is and its altitude, he'll tell you that too or he may not give you the traffic report at all, if he's certain there's no potential danger. There are three possible acknowledgements:

If you're in the clouds, say so: "45 Juliet's in the clouds" or "45 Juliet's on the gauges". Obviously, the traffic is VFR at some other altitude (you hope the fellow is legal) or it's IFR under some other controller (unlikely because then it would be well separated from you and your controller would not call it out).

If you're in VFR conditions, you have to look for the traffic. After a few seconds, if you don't see it (probably at another altitude), acknowledge: "45 Juliet looking." And keep looking. It might just loom up in your windscreen even though you didn't see it a few seconds earlier. Remember also that the controller gives you the direction of the traffic with reference to your track on his radar scope; he has no idea how you may be crabbing into the wind. So you have to compensate for this when you look out. "One o'clock" would mean to look straight ahead (12 o'clock) if you were crabbing 30 degrees to the right. If you were crabbing 30 degrees to the left, the same call would mean to look all the way around to the right at your 2 o'clock position. When the traffic is no longer of concern because it has passed by, or your courses clearly don't converge, ATC will tell you: "45 Juliet clear of traffic." Acknowledge: "45 Juliet, thank you."

Finally, **if you spot the traffic** (and this sometimes really happens and you silently thank the system), acknowledge: "45 Juliet, contact" or "45 Juliet, we have the traffic."

Position Reports. Nowadays, with radar coverage over so much of the country, position reports are no longer as important as they used to be, when ATC depended upon them for following the progress of your flight. Nevertheless, there are still many situations in which you will have to make position reports. You could be out of radar range, especially at low altitudes in many parts of the country. Your transponder could be inoperative, or ATC radar could be out of commission. So you should know and practice the correct professional way to make a position report.

The report follows a logical sequence (**PTA TEN** is the memory aid), and it has a natural rhythm to it. First, of course, you identify yourself. Then you say where you were (**Position**) and when you were there (**Time**) in minutes past the hour. Next you say your **Altitude** and the **Type** of flight plan, in this case IFR. Then comes your **Estimate** at the next reporting point (and of course you name it). Finally, you give the name of the **Next** reporting point beyond that. So the report, once you have identified yourself, has four simple parts to it. For easy intelligible delivery, you should drop your voice after each of these parts.

Suppose you've just passed FISH intersection at 18 past the hour, you are flying at 7000 feet, your ETA at DODGE VOR is at 41 past the hour, and the subsequent reporting point after DODGE is HILLS VOR. Here is how the entire report would go:

> You: "Seattle Center, Cherokee 2345 Juliet at FISH." You have alerted him to expect a position report by saying the name of the reporting point.
> ATC: "2345 Juliet, Seattle Center."
> You: "45 Juliet at FISH, 18. ("one eight"). (Pause) DODGE at 41 ("four one"). (Pause) HILLS."
> ATC: "Thank you, 45 Juliet. Report DODGE."
> You: "Report DODGE. 45 Juliet."

If HILLS were at your destination, you would say DESTINATION instead of naming it, to verify with the controller that you will be terminating the flight there—presumably by starting an IFR approach at the HILLS VOR.

"Pop-up" Filing. Often you'll start off on a long crosscountry flight in good VFR conditions only to find along the way that the weather is deteriorating. You can try to maintain VFR by keeping contact with the terrain, but this means going down and risking a squeeze between lowering ceilings and the ground—even more risky if the terrain is rising. Another choice is to climb to VFR-on-top, but then you risk not finding any way down again at your destination, or worse—especially without oxygen aboard—being forced higher and higher if the tops rise along your route. Without an IFR rating your only really safe alternative may be to do a 180 and land somewhere in good weather. But with your IFR rating the solution is simple: you just get IFR clearance from wherever you are to wherever you're going. This is called a "pop-up" because from the controller's point of view, you just suddenly appear there; even in an area with radar coverage, before you call you're just another anonymous VFR flight squawking 1200 on the radar scope. The procedure for obtaining a "pop-up" clearance is surprisingly simple, and the clearance can usually be obtained immediately or with only slight delay while you maintain VFR.

First locate yourself properly on the IFR chart with reference to a known airway and VOR or intersection. Then call and tell ATC where you are and what you want. For this you'll need the discrete sector frequency for the area you are flying in. This is shown on the IFR enroute charts, and if you can't find it there, you can always call FSS through the nearest VOR (transmit on 122.1, listen on the omni) and ask for the appropriate frequency.

Example: You: "Oakland Center, Cherokee 2345 Juliet."
ATC: "Cherokee 2345 Juliet, Oakland Center."
You: "45 Juliet on the 060 radial from Linden, 23 DME, at four thousand five hundred VFR squawking 1200. Request IFR clearance to San Jose."
ATC: "45 Juliet squawk 1163 and ident."
You: Do it.
ATC: "45 Juliet radar contact 21 miles northeast of Linden. Cleared to the San Jose airport via direct Linden, Victor 113 Stockton, Victor 244 South Sunol, Victor 334 San Jose. Maintain 6000."
You: "45 Juliet cleared direct Linden, Victor 113 Stockton, Victor 244 South Sunol, Victor 334 San Jose, maintain 6000. And we're leaving four point five for six."
ATC: "Readback correct, report level at six thousand."
You: "Report level at 6. 45 Juliet."

You climb into the clouds and settle back. The worry and uncertainty of a few minutes ago have vanished, and your flight continues smoothly to its destination.

Is ATC Still There? The Lost Communications Problem. On a busy frequency, as you bore through the clouds, you have the comforting reassurance of hearing the controller handling other traffic. You know you can reach him in a moment should you have to. But sometimes, when not much is going on, there are long long silences. It is important to understand when this may be cause for worry. In IFR cruise on your IFR flight plan, you don't really need to talk to ATC at all. Indeed, if you lost radio communications altogether, you'd still know how to proceed smoothly and without concern to complete your flight according to plan, right through the final approach and landing at your destination airport. The rules are all carefully spelled out, and you'll follow them, and ATC will know you're following them, and will act accordingly to clear your path and assure your proper separation from other IFR aircraft.

With radar vectors, on the other hand, you are in a tricky situation. You'll notice that whenever you get radar vectors, the controller will explain their purpose; for example, "Fly heading 225, radar vectors to Mission intersection". The purpose is to tell you what to do if you should lose two-way communications. You would just get to Mission on your own navigation, and proceed from there according to your flight plan. But how do you know when you've lost communications? Here is where you have to stay alert. First, you need to know something about the terrain. Whenever you are on a radar vector that would take you into a dangerous situation if continued indefinitely, you should not hesitate to call the controller if you don't hear from him for an inordinately long time. This can be done very courteously—you can even make up some excuse for conversation (asking for a time check or a transponder check is a good innocent way to get an answer). Using your cockpit timer is also wise. Start it at a known point where the radar vector started; then you'll always know from the elapsed time and your airspeed approximately where you've gotten to, and thus you can monitor your progress. If the terrain ahead is at 5000 feet and 15 miles away, while you are being vectored at 3000 feet and making 100 knots, you should certainly be concerned after 5 minutes or so if the radio remains silent. If your receiver or the controller's transmitter has given up the ghost, now is the time to find out about it. And if you really can't communicate, you'll want to initiate lost communications procedures before it's too late.

In situations like the above, the controller will often anticipate the problem. For example: "2345 Juliet turn right heading 225, radar vectors to Mission intersection. If no communications for 15 seconds, proceed direct Mission." This type of command is also typical of the precision radar approach (PAR, or GCA). On final, you will always hear something like: "If you receive no transmission for 5 seconds, execute an immediate missed approach." This is your guarantee against flying into the ground if your radio fails during the approach.

Finally, beware of accepting a clearance to a destination airport that has no published IFR approach, unless you are absolutely certain the weather will be CAVU when you get there. Even then, be sure you have filed an alternate, which, of course, will have a published approach. Here is an example of the problem. Palo Alto airport has no IFR approach. Suppose you file a flight plan via Victor airways to Woodside VOR (9 miles from Palo Alto) thence to Palo Alto as destination, and ATC clears you accordingly. As you approach Woodside, you are given radar vectors to Palo Alto, the intention being to vector you down from 5000 (where you are) to 2000 (the minimum vectoring altitude in this area). The ceiling at Palo Alto is overcast at 3000 feet. On paper it looks all right. But what do you do if you have communications failure? Where do you go, at what altitude, and how do you get there? And how do you ever get safely down? The solution to this problem is never to accept vectors in such a situation without a clear alternative in case of communications failure. Indeed, the original flight plan should have specified an alternate airport with an IFR approach (e.g., San Jose, which is 15 miles from Palo Alto). Then you could safely request and accept vectors to Palo Alto, knowing (and ATC knowing) that in case of communications failure you would proceed to San Jose, make the approach, and then either land there or proceed VFR to Palo Alto.

Practice.

The time to practice your communications skills is when you are not flying the airplane. In addition to listening—spend a lot of time listening to the radio and following what's going on—you should fly imaginary IFR flights, in the comfort of your own home, and say out loud your responses to various imagined ATC transmissions. You may feel silly at first, but the only way to learn crisp communications is to practice them over and over, out loud, listening to how you sound, and trying to improve your delivery and intelligibility every time. A tape recorder can be an excellent aid; use it freely, both for your own preliminary practice sessions and in the serious practice sessions described below.

When you are thoroughly familiar with the material in this chapter, have a session with your check pilot friend. Work with an actual IFR enroute chart. Lay it out on the table in front of you, and have your friend start by giving you a clearance to copy for a simulated IFR flight. It should be read slowly in the early sessions, faster as you become more proficient. It is best in all these exercises if your check pilot is IFR rated, so that the clearances and instructions, on the ground and in the air, will be close to the real thing. An alternative for this exercise in communications would be for your instructor to write down or tape record a set of clearances, from which you could work.

Make sure that in each practice session your check pilot surprises you with various revised clearances, simulated emergencies, loss of communications, etc., to test your coolness and efficiency in dealing with each problem. Some simulated flights should start out VFR, to test your proficiency at pop-up filing.

Here is an example of how a typical practice session should go. All the details to fill up a number of sessions like this have to be invented and planned well beforehand by your check pilot or instructor. In this session let's lay out an IFR flight from San Jose, California to Reno, Nevada, using the appropriate low altitude enroute chart. Fig. 3-1 gives a section of the Enroute Chart appropriate to the first portion of this trip. Your friend, as usual, will play the role of ATC controller.

Ground Control: "Cherokee 2345 Juliet, clearance."
You: "45 Juliet, ready to copy."
GC: "Cherokee 2345 Juliet is cleared to the Reno Airport via Victor 334 Sacramento, Victor 6 Reno. Maintain 5000. On departure turn right, heading 035 to intercept Victor 334. Departure control frequency will be 121.3. Squawk 1141 on departure."
You: "45 Juliet, stand by." Then check the clearance against your

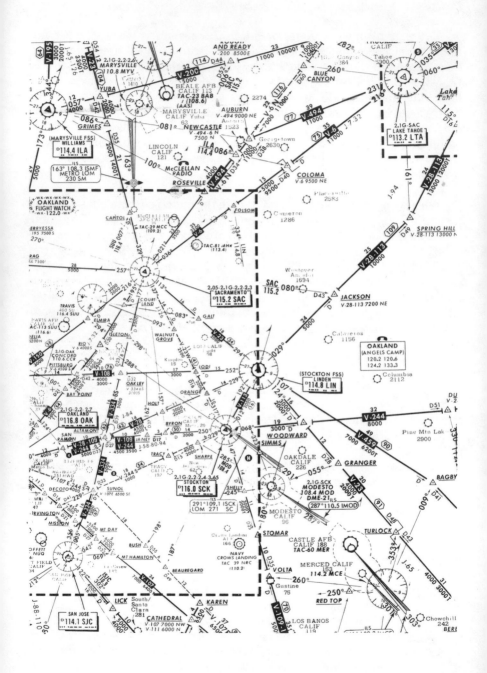

Fig. 3-1

GC: "Readback correct 45 Juliet."

You: On tower frequency when you're ready. "45 Juliet ready to go."

Tower: "45 Juliet hold for departure release."

You: "45 Juliet."

T: "45 Juliet cleared for takeoff."

You: Acknowledge, make sure your transponder is on, write down the time, and roll onto the runway.

T: (When you're airborne and climbing out): "45 Juliet contact departure control, have a good flight."

You: "Thank you, 45 Juliet." (Now on 121.3) "Bay Departure Control, 45 Juliet airborne San Jose, climbing to 5."

Departure Control: "45 Juliet, radar contact 1 mile northwest of the San Jose airport, report passing 2000."

You: "Report out of 2. 45 Juliet." (And a few minutes later) "45 Juliet leaving two thousand."

DC: "Roger 45 Juliet. Report reaching 5000."

You: "Report at 5. 45 Juliet."

DC: "Cherokee 2345 Juliet radar contact lost 15 miles north of San Jose. Resume normal navigation. Report Oakley intersection.

You: "45 Juliet resuming normal navigation. Report Oakley .... And we're just level at 5."

DC: "Roger 45 Juliet. Contact Oakland Center on 120.6."

You: "120.6 now. Thank you and good evening." Then switch to the new frequency, and listen, then check in with the new controller: "Oakland Center, 45 Juliet with you at 5000."

Oakland Center: "45 Juliet Ident."

You: Do it.

OC: "Negative transponder return, 45 Juliet. Squawk Standby."

You: Do it (i.e., switch your transponder to the standby position).

OC: "45 Juliet squawk 1100 normal." He's trying to see if your transponder will work on another code.

You: Do it. Change the code to 1100, and switch to ON.

OC: "Negative radar contact, 45 Juliet. Continue normal navigation. Report Oakley."

You: "Report Oakley. 45 Juliet."

You should have noted the time at takeoff, so you know when to start watching closely for Oakley intersection. One VOR is set on Sacramento VOR, 357 degrees inbound (Victor 334). Your second VOR is tuned to Linden with OBS set to 252 degrees, the radial that defines Oakley intersection; your needle on this VOR points to the right (toward Linden) before you reach Oakley, and it will cross over, to point away from Linden once you have passed the intersection. Let's suppose your true airspeed is 120 knots and that winds aloft were forecast to be light and variable up to 9000 feet. Then, since Oakley is 44 miles from San Jose, you can expect to be there in 22 minutes plus the time for your climb at reduced airspeed, say 25 minutes in all. If your takeoff was at 8:07 p.m. local time, you can expect to be at Oakley around 8:32. Sure enough, just on time the needle crosses the center line. Don't be overeager to tell your good news to ATC. Write down your time at Oakley. Then compute your ETA for the next compulsory reporting point, which is Sacramento VOR. It is 23 miles from Oakley, so you estimate Sacramento at 32 minutes past the hour (the time at Oakley) plus 11 minutes (always ignore fractions of a minute), or 43. Write it down. Then look at the chart and find the next reporting point after Sacramento. Lake Tahoe VOR is not compulsory, and the one after that is Reno, your destination, not shown in Fig. 3-1. Then call Center.

OC: "2345 Juliet, Oakland Center."
You: "45 Juliet at Oakley, 32. (Slight pause) 5000 IFR. (Slight pause). Sacramento at 43. (Slight pause) Destination."
OC: "Roger, 45 Juliet. Ident."
You: Do it.
OC: "45 Juliet, I still have no transponder return on you. Report Sacramento."
You: "Report Sacramento. 45 Juliet."

At 43 minutes past the hour the TO-FROM indicator is still showing TO Sacramento, but 2 minutes later you get the TO-FROM reversal. Don't call ATC. Fly the airplane first. You have to fly outbound on Victor 6, which follows the 036 radial. So, as you cross the VOR, start a right turn to 056 (a 20-degree intercept, since you are so close to the station) and at the same time, rotate the OBS to the outbound course, 036. The needle will be to your right, because that's where the chosen course is, and as you intercept it, it will center, and you'll roll out on 036. Now call in your report: "45 Juliet at Sacramento, 45 (slight pause), 5000 (slight pause), destination at 23 (you made this calculation before you called)." Saying "IFR" is often omitted if it is obvious.

OC: "Roger 45 Juliet. Climb and maintain 10,000 (one zero thousand). Expect 11,000 (one one thousand) at Folsom."
You: "45 Juliet is leaving five thousand for one zero thousand. Expect one one thousand at Folsom."

And start your climb. The controller wants you at 11,000 feet at a particular segment of your route, possibly because he has traffic coming in the opposite direction, say at 10,000 feet. He wants you above the conflicting traffic in ample time, and he tells you when to expect it in the event of communications failure. If you had such a failure before you reached Folsom, you'd just climb to 11,000 at Folsom.

And so the remainder of the flight continues, over the mountains, over to another Center frequency, then to an Approach Controller at Reno, eventually to a safe landing after the ILS approach at Reno. Maybe you can get your transponder fixed before your next flight.

Scoring on practice exercises of this type is largely a matter of your check pilot being knowledgeable and alert, so that every error you make can be scored and pointed out. In order not to fatigue you, and to keep the sessions comparable for scoring purposes, the check pilot should limit each session to 30 minutes. The score sheet gives the main categories of error. Each and every error should be scored either 10 or 20 points, depending on whether it is a minor slip or lack of finesse, or whether it is an error that could cause serious trouble or significant delay in complying with a clearance. Zero points on this score sheet will indicate a crisp, confident, professional kind of communication ability. Now, as you concentrate on sharpening your IFR flying skills, communication should become second nature to you, and not distract you from the main job.

Score Sheet

Session:	1	2	3	4	5	6	7	8	9	10
Date:										
ITEM Generally sluggish, hesitant, or confused responses to ATC Instructions. (10 or 20 points)										
Position reports—errors or lack of smooth delivery. (10 or 20 points)										
Pop-up filing—errors or confusion. (10 or 20 points)										
Lost communications procedures—uncertainty about how to proceed, or actual errors in proceeding on correct course. (10 or 20 points)										
TOTAL SCORE FOR 30-MINUTE EXERCISE										

4.   PRINCIPLES OF IFR FLYING

The Five Basic Principles.

The key to safe and efficient flight under IFR conditions is smoothness. And the key to smoothness lies in knowing exactly what to do to maintain a given flight condition and what to do (and in what order) to change to a different flight condition. By "flight condition" we mean a complete description of what the airplane is doing. For example: "Cruising flight, level at 5000 feet, airspeed 100 knots, heading 160" is a flight condition. "Descent at 500 feet per minute, airspeed 80 knots, in a standard rate turn from heading 160 to 250" is another flight condition.

Principle 1. Every desired flight condition is established and maintained by choosing a particular combination of pitch, power, and bank.

The role of bank is pretty obvious. All turns of 30 degrees or more are executed at standard rate. Turns of less than 30 degrees require a less rapid rate of turn, and therefore a lesser degree of bank; the usual rule for small aircraft is to use half as much bank as the degrees of turn desired, thus 10 degrees of bank for 20 degrees of turn, 5 degrees of bank for 10 degrees of turn. Smaller changes of heading are accomplished by very slight bank, or even—as some advocate on localizer approaches—by slight rudder pressure (i.e., skidding slightly instead of banking).

The roles of pitch and power are the subject of heated controversy. Of course, it is the **combination** of pitch and power (or more exactly, of angle of attack and power) that determines whether the airplane will climb, fly level, or descend, and at what airspeed. From a **theoretical** standpoint it makes no sense to say that "pitch controls airspeed and power controls altitude change" (which is what we are going to say anyway) or conversely, that "pitch controls altitude change and power controls airspeed". In one of the really classic expositions of the principles of flight, Langewiesche in his famous *STICK AND RUDDER* (McGraw-Hill Book Co., 1944) discusses this age-old controversy and shows clearly why there is only one **practical** answer to it, as given in Principle 2.

Principle 2. Pitch attitude determines airspeed, and power determines altitude change.

At any given airspeed, power determines what the airplane will do. Consider a small airplane flying at 80 knots. At a certain power setting— perhaps 2200 RPM, you will be in level flight at a moderately high angle of attack. At the same airspeed with full power you will be nearly at a maximum rate of climb, having raised the nose to a higher angle of attack to keep the airspeed at 80. If you reduce the power to 1700 RPM, the nose will drop and a moderate descent will begin, still at 80 knots. Cutting the power to idle will let the nose drop still more and you will be in a normal glide at 80 knots. The same principle holds at all airspeeds except very near the stall, on the back side of the power curve, where maximum power will be required to fly level, and therefore no climb is possible. You don't really want your airspeed changing except when you want to change, so you set your **airspeed** by choosing the appropriate pitch, and then use whatever power is needed to climb, fly level, or descend at the required rate. The shortcut way of describing this method of control is to say that the **elevator** (i.e., the yoke) **controls the airspeed**.

Langewiesche points out that you could make permanent marks on the column of your yoke, showing the various airspeeds in the airplane's working range—e.g., 60 knots when the yoke is nearly all the way back, 70, 80, 90, and so on, for yoke positions farther and farther forward. This will not work exactly under all flight conditions, but it is pretty close. It is related to the fact that very little trim change is needed for different power settings at the same airspeed. As pointed out earlier, the nose tends to respond automatically to power changes in such a way that the airspeed remains approximately constant. This is due to the aerodynamic longitudinal stability of the airplane. If you are flying level at 100 knots and reduce power, the nose will drop, reducing the angle of attack, and the reduced lift will result in a descent. Conversely, increasing power will tend to raise the nose, increasing the angle of attack, increasing lift, so that the airplane climbs. Changing flight conditions at constant airspeed, therefore, requires little retrimming— the airplane virtually flies itself, **trimmed for a given airspeed**.

Principle 3. In coordinated flight (ball centered), the aircraft will fly a constant heading if the wings are level; and it will turn if the wings are banked, at a rate of turn determined by the angle of bank and the airspeed.

It follows from this principle that the most important single device for IFR flight is an instrument that will tell you when your wings are level. There is absolutely no way to "feel" whether or not you are in a bank, since in a coordinated turn the G forces act vertically with respect to you, regardless of where the ground is. In Chapter 1 you learned how to prove this to yourself through special disorientation exercises. Fortunately, you have several instruments to give you the correct information: your attitude indicator (AI), your directional gyro (DG), your turn needle powered independently of the other gyro instruments, on certain headings your magnetic compass, and even your ADF. A most valuable accessory for IFR flight is a simple automatic wing leveller (a single-axis autopilot), which will maintain a heading reasonably well by simply restoring the wings-level condition whenever it is disturbed.

Principle 4. The instruments used to establish a desired flight condition are called control instruments. The instruments used to monitor and maintain a desired flight condition are called monitoring instruments.

This terminology is different from that used by FAA in their INSTRUMENT FLYING HANDBOOK. I think it is more accurate and less confusing than the FAA terms, "primary instruments" and "supporting instruments". The basic procedure for establishing a new flight condition consists of two distinct sequential steps. **First,** a definite change is established on a control instrument. **Then,** the appropriate monitoring instrument is observed to see if you've accomplished your objective. If not, you make a small adjustment by means of the control instrument, then check the monitoring instrument again. And you repeat the process until you get it just right.

Let's take an example—setting up a standard rate turn. You know about how much bank will be required, and you set up that degree of bank with ailerons, using the AI as your control instrument. Now you look at the turn needle, which is your monitoring instrument for rate of turn. If the rate of turn is too great or too small, you correct with ailerons, changing the bank angle by a definite small amount on the AI, then again monitor the turn needle.

Another example is setting up a definite rate of descent—say 500 feet per minute—at cruise airspeed. You throttle back to an RPM setting you know from experience should be about right; here your tachometer (or manifold pressure gauge) is the control instrument for power (altitude change). Then, keeping the airspeed constant with small pitch changes if required, you monitor the descent on your vertical speed indicator (VSI). If the descent is too slow or too fast, you make a small change of power and monitor again. The basis of the whole procedure is to set up a condition and then to monitor it, and then to make small corrections if necessary.

A final example is from the realm of navigation. You wish to track a VOR radial inbound to the station, as you might do in an IFR approach. Your DG is the control instrument for heading; you set up a definite heading on it. But the primary control instrument for maintaining a heading is always the AI. Hold the wings level, with the index **exactly** aligned in the center, and your heading will automatically be held. The center of your attention remains the AI, and you only glance at the DG from time to time to make sure the heading is correct. Then you can also glance at the VOR needle to see how you are doing. The VOR indicator is the monitoring instrument, but be careful not to fly the needle. If the needle deviates, you change the heading (on the DG) toward the needle by a small definite amount, by making a small bank on the AI. Then continue monitoring the needle occasionally. This two-step procedure applies to every change in flight condition. It produces smoothness and reliability, with minimum effort. The alternative is to "chase the needle"—meaning to overcorrect, then overcorrect in the other direction, resulting in an airplane always somewhat out of control, with airspeed varying, altitude varying, heading varying, and pilot working too hard to keep things going right.

Principle 5. Virtually all IFR flight may be regarded as a series of maneuvers at constant airspeed.

The "numbers" that are critical for every airplane are airspeeds: the stall speeds in different configurations, the best rate and best angle climb speeds, normal cruise, the best glide speed, the initial approach speed, and the final approach speed. Thus, the airspeed is chosen deliberately by the pilot—it doesn't just happen. Even a constant-rate climb or descent is a special case of the constant airspeed maneuver, in which the airspeed is chosen first, and then the desired vertical rate is determined by the power setting.

The Instruments and Their Functions.

Pitch Instruments. The only direct pitch control instrument is the AI. This is the control instrument for establishing a desired pitch attitude, by placing the small airplane a certain amount above or below (or on) the artificial horizon. Deviations are measured in bar widths (half bar high, two bars low, etc.). The most accurate reference point on this instrument is the small dot in the center of the little airplane. In cruising level flight at normal cruise power setting with altimeter and VSI stable, the position of this little dot should be adjusted so it is exactly on the horizon. The adjustment made on the ground, in the runup area, may not be quite precise, since the pitch attitude in level flight may not be exactly the same as on the ground, indeed, it is different for every airspeed.

The monitoring instrument for pitch is the airspeed indicator, but the VSI is an invaluable adjunct. In level flight, the VSI is extremely sensitive to small pitch changes, since with constant power an increase in pitch attitude initiates a climb, and a decrease initiates a descent. While the ASI is subject to lag because of the momentum of the aircraft (it takes time for it to slow down or speed up), the VSI gives an instantaneous indication of departure from level flight. If the AI is inoperative (under "partial panel" conditions, as with gyro failure), both the ASI and VSI are used as control and monitoring instruments for pitch. At cruise power setting, maintaining a constant airspeed and neutral position of the VSI with appropriate yoke pressures (or trim) will ensure level flight by maintaining a constant pitch attitude.

Power Instruments. The manifold pressure gauge (MP) or tachometer (with a fixed-pitch prop) is the control instrument for power. Throttle is used to establish the desired reading on this instrument. Unexpected changes in manifold pressure or RPM are signs of trouble, such as carburetor icing or incorrect mixture.

The altimeter and vertical speed indicator are monitoring instruments for power. In level flight, if the airspeed is correct but the altimeter and VSI show a climb or descent, power has to be adjusted accordingly. However, above the altitude at which full throttle is required for cruise power, no power increase is possible, and any indication of a descent has to be countered by an increase in pitch (at the expense of airspeed) in order to maintain level flight. This would be the situation, for example, in down drafts at altitude. In descents, the VSI is the monitoring instrument for power; the desired rate of descent is obtained by fine adjustment of power, as in establishing a constant rate of descent on an IFR approach.

Bank Instruments. The AI is the control instrument for bank. It is the only instrument that indicates bank directly. If the AI is inoperative, the turn needle becomes the control instrument for bank; the ball must be centered.

The DG is the usual monitoring instrument for bank. In straight flight the heading is held constant, and small deviations in heading are corrected promptly with very slight coordinated aileron and rudder movements (some prefer slight rudder pressure alone for correcting very small deviations). In turning flight, the rate of turn is monitored on the turn needle, and the DG is also monitored in order to roll out smoothly on the new heading.

For a desired rate of turn—usually a standard rate turn—the turn needle is the monitoring instrument, with the DG as accessory monitoring instrument, as described above. If no vacuum operated gyro instruments are working, the electrically operated needle becomes both control and monitoring instrument for bank, the rollout to the new heading is monitored by the clock (timed turns) and the new heading is verified by the magnetic compass after the rollout.

If no gyro instruments are operative, the magnetic compass can be used as a monitoring instrument for bank. This is difficult, however, because on all but southerly headings the movements of the magnetic compass are difficult to interpret, and may even (near northerly headings) be momentarily opposite to the direction of turn. On southerly headings the magnetic compass can be used to monitor straight flight and small changes of heading; it is very sensitive to small amounts of turn and therefore to small degrees of bank, and thus acts as an effective wings-level indicator. In extreme emergency the ADF, tuned to a station straight ahead or astern, will also serve as a monitoring instrument for straight wings-level flight.

The Basic Maneuvers.

The use of the instruments is illustrated by the four basic maneuvers; these are incorporated into the exercises presented in the next few chapters. Here the main principles are outlined.

1. Straight and level flight. We want to fly straight and level at a specified airspeed, perhaps normal cruise, perhaps some slower speed. The problem is to establish the desired airspeed and find by trial and error what power setting is needed to fly level. The two monitoring instruments used to maintain level flight are the altimeter and the VSI. Since we undoubtedly wish to fly level at a given altitude (for example, the altitude assigned by ATC), the altimeter is the chief monitoring instrument. But the VSI has a very important function—it is a sensitive trend instrument, showing immediately that we are about to climb or descend from the assigned altitude. Careful observation of the VSI, therefore, permits us to make corrections even before the deviations are observed on the altimeter. Small deviations (less than 50 feet) from the desired altitude can be compensated most easily by small pitch corrections. Indeed, the slightest movement of the VSI can be counteracted by tiny control pressures exerted with the thumb or fingers on the yoke, so that the altimeter never shows a significant deviation at all. If, through inattentiveness, an altitude deviation of greater than 50 feet is permitted to develop, it should be corrected immediately by a small power change. The secret of altitude control, therefore, is to scan the VSI and altimeter constantly, and to respond promptly but gently to very small deviations, in order to avoid the sloppy technique of making large corrections by throttle juggling after large deviations develop.

Since straight flight means wings-level flight at a specified heading, the DG is the monitoring instrument for straight flight. At every moment in an IFR flight, unless you are **turning** to a new and definite heading, you are **holding** a definite heading. Your check pilot should be able to ask you at any time, "What is your heading supposed to be?" and receive an immediate reply. If you don't know what heading you're supposed to be flying, there's no way you can keep the airplane under proper control in IFR conditions. This is especially true in IFR approaches, where the heading has to be held within a degree or two all the way inbound from the final approach fix. If you are holding 305 degrees, and keep it firmly in mind, you won't tolerate 307 or 303, but you'll make tiny corrections as soon as the first deviation occurs. The principle is the same as with altitude control: you have to make small corrections to small deviations, in order to avoid making large corrections after large deviations develop. Alternatives for heading control when the DG is inoperative were discussed earlier.

   2. Turns to headings. All turns in IFR flight are standard rate or slower. Turns of 30 degrees or more are at standard rate, smaller turns are at a slower rate (lesser degree of bank). You know approximately the angle of bank required for a standard rate turn at a given airspeed in your airplane. For most small aircraft at cruise airspeed this is about 15-20 degrees. The first step, then, in initiating a turn, is to establish the angle of bank on the AI—the only instrument that gives a direct indication of the angle of bank. Then immediately turn your attention to the turn needle, which is the monitoring instrument throughout the turn. If it shows other than a perfect standard rate turn, change the bank angle slightly (using the AI) then scan the turn needle again. During the turn, monitor the DG. The DG is the monitoring instrument for completion of the turn and rollout on the new heading; remember to lead the rollout—usually by about 10 degrees. If the DG is inoperative, the clock becomes the monitoring instrument. At standard rate, you divide the number of degrees of heading change to be accomplished by 3, to get the number of seconds of turn, since you are turning 3 degrees per second. After the rollout, you let the magnetic compass settle down, and see if the new heading is correct. If not, small timed turns are made to correct it. Finally, if the clock is also inoperative, the magnetic compass itself becomes the monitoring instrument for the entire turn. Then attention must be paid to the special requirements for leading or lagging the rollout, depending upon whether you are turning to a northerly or a southerly heading.

   It is essential, during turns, to scan the AI, VSI and altimeter, to ensure against inadvertent climbs or descents. A descent during a turn results from the natural tendency of the nose to drop; because of the loss of lift due to banking of the wings, some back pressure is needed to maintain level flight. The small dot in the center of the simulated airplane on the AI should simply be kept in its constant position on the artificial horizon throughout the turn. A climb during a turn is due to overcontrolling; usually you'll find that your hand is gripping the yoke too tightly, so just relax it.

   3. Climbs. There are only three kinds of climb: **maximum angle** (which concerns you only for obstacle clearance during takeoff), **maximum rate** (which you'll use most often, and always during missed approaches), and **cruise climb.** Since each kind of climb has its own specific airspeed in a given aircraft, all the climbs are simply constant airspeed maneuvers. The correct pitch attitude is first established on the AI, then the climb is monitored on the ASI to obtain the correct airspeed, and the power is set to climb power on the MP gauge or tachometer. Starting the climb is a two-step procedure. First, raise the pitch attitude on the AI, and wait for the airspeed to fall to the desired climb airspeed. Then bring in climb power. Thus, you first trade off airspeed for climb performance, then sustain the climb by the necessary power. Levelling off from a climb is also a two-step procedure. When the desired altitude is reached on the altimeter, briskly reduce the pitch on the AI to that required for level flight, and keep it there (this will require increasing yoke pressure as the airspeed builds up). Monitor the increasing airspeed on the ASI, and when it reaches cruise, reduce the power to the proper cruise power setting. Finally, trim as required to maintain level flight. This maneuver is the reverse of instituting a climb. Here we trade off pitch for airspeed, with constant monitoring of the altimeter to avoid further climb or a dive.

4. Descents. As described under **Principle 5**, all descents are also constant airspeed maneuvers. Enroute descents are executed at cruise airspeed. Power is simply reduced to the setting that is known to give the desired rate of descent on the VSI. This usually requires virtually no trim change; as the power is reduced, the nose will drop a little, the airspeed will be maintained, and the descent will begin. To level off at the desired altitude, briskly return the power to the cruise setting, and continue to maintain cruise airspeed. The very same principles apply to approaches, except that a lower airspeed is used, and therefore the airplane has to be retrimmed to a higher angle of attack. In small aircraft, when levelling off from both climbs and descents, there is usually no need to lead the altimeter; when the desired altitude is reached, prompt reduction or application of power to the level flight setting results in immediate stopping of the altimeter movement.

In the next chapters these basic maneuvers will be elaborated into a set of practice exercises, first one by one, then in combination. When they have all been mastered, you will be proficient in the elements of IFR flying. Only when you can fly the airplane smoothly under IFR conditions, without effort, can you start to handle the other essential tasks, like navigation, communication, and record keeping.

5. STRAIGHT AND LEVEL. TURNS TO HEADINGS.

Full Panel.

Principles. This exercise aims to develop your skill at maintaining altitude while you hold a definite heading and maintaining that same altitude while you turn smoothly and precisely to a new heading. First you'll do it with full panel, then with partial panel. A word of warning: It is tempting to do IFR practice alone—not under the hood—but ostensibly VFR while you actually fly on the instruments. Don't. It's both unsafe and illegal, for you can't possibly give your attention to the "see and be seen" concept with your head down and absorbed with the gauges. Always have a qualified pilot riding with you in the right seat, who can give his attention to scanning for traffic, while you, properly under the hood, can give your attention to the IFR exercise. As you progress, however, you'll find that you apply more and more IFR technique to your VFR flying, scanning back and forth from outside to the instruments. This is indeed appropriate, and very good practice for real IFR flying, which has often to be conducted just like that—when you're not in the clouds and you're therefore responsible for collision avoidance, and when you transition from an actual IFR approach to the runway environment just before landing. As you apply this mixed IFR-VFR technique, you'll be surprised at how your VFR flying improves, and your passengers will be pleased at the smoothness of the ride.

Now, with your check pilot in the right seat and your hood firmly in place, you'll climb to a safe altitude, say 3000 feet above terrain. Set up cruise power and airspeed, and trim the airplane very carefully; fine trim, so you can virtually fly hands off, is the secret of success. Establish a definite heading and fly straight and level. Your primary reference instruments are the DG for heading, and the altimeter for altitude. Let your scan take in the AI (adjust it so the little dot is exactly on the horizon) and the ASI (note carefully your indicated airspeed in this level-flight cruising condition with the given fixed power setting). Hold the yoke very lightly with your left thumb and two fingers. Now your work begins.

Suppose your heading is 165. As you scan, try to catch the very earliest small deviation in heading and correct it at once with **very slight** bank, no more than a degree or two. As your scan takes in the altimeter, catch the very slightest deviation here too. The smallest division on the altimeter is 20 feet; if you deviate that much, correct it at once: very slight thumb pressure to lose excess altitude, very slight pull with your fingers to gain lost altitude. Don't become preoccupied with one instrument. If you become too engrossed in the altimeter, your heading will surely wander; if you stare at the DG, you'll be certain to lose or gain altitude.

Some pilots find it easy to use the index at the top of the AI as the main heading reference. This is a very accurate indicator of the wings-level condition—more accurate than merely leveling the wings of the small airplane against the horizon. But even so, you must scan the DG frequently to be sure the heading remains exactly what it should be. If the ball is not centered, you can keep the wings perfectly level and your heading will still drift systematically, since you will be in a continuous slight skid; so be sure rudder trim (if you have it) as well as elevator trim is correct. Also don't forget to check periodically for precession of the DG; it doesn't help much to hold a perfect heading if it's the wrong heading.

The main cause of altitude deviation is imperfect elevator trim. If you keep gaining or losing consistently, adjust the trim. Another cause of altitude deviation is tension in your left hand; here the tendency is to pull on the yoke, so you should suspect this if you keep gaining altitude despite good trim. Finally, you will certainly gain and lose altitude as you encounter up and down drafts. This is a bit tricky. If the changes are small, you should react to them as you do to any deviation, by gently pushing or pulling the yoke. But this technique is no good with severe up and down drafts, such as you get in really turbulent conditions. If you try to fight the turbulence, you'll be raising the nose excessively one minute (with a severe and possibly dangerous loss of airspeed) and diving the next (with the airspeed needle running into the yellow). In general, what goes up has to come down, and all the air can't go up or down simultaneously, so it is best to maintain a constant pitch attitude and let things average out over time. Despite the momentary ups and downs, you'll be surprised at how little you really deviate from the assigned altitude. Updrafts will alternate with downdrafts. On the other hand, you can't accept deviations running into the hundreds of feet, or you'll be violating your ATC clearance. Therefore, if the ups and downs are that bad, use power changes to compensate, while maintaining a nearly normal pitch attitude. Reduce power if you're high, increase power if you're low. A good general rule is to make a power adjustment whenever you deviate more than 50 feet from the assigned altitude. As pointed out earlier, if you already have full throttle, you will have to climb by increasing pitch at the expense of airspeed.

Turns to headings are simple. Turns of more than 30 degrees are always standard rate, lesser turns require lesser degrees of bank. In most small aircraft at ordinary cruise airspeeds the standard rate turn requires a bank angle of 15-20 degrees. As you roll into the turn your primary instrument is the AI, on which you set up what you know to be the correct bank for your airplane. Then move your gaze to the turn indicator, which will be your monitoring instrument during the turn. Make very small bank adjustments to put the turn indicator right on the standard rate mark. Then move your scan to the DG to watch the progress of the turn, scanning back and forth from the turn indicator to the DG until it's time to start the rollout. Lead the rollout by about 10 degrees, as you learned to do earlier in your flying career. Make the rollout very smooth, and finally roll out exactly on the new heading. Smoothness is what you are striving for. Throughout the turn you must include the altimeter in your scan so that you can use just the right amount of back pressure to counteract the slight loss of lift, and release the back pressure as you roll out.

The difference between an inexperienced pilot and a pro is in the smoothness of turns in IFR conditions. The key to doing it right is attention to the angle of bank as shown on the AI. This is why it is important to know the exact bank angle for a standard rate turn at cruise airspeed. The initial roll-in is precise, to exactly the right bank angle, coordinating rudder and aileron, followed by prompt neutralization of the controls to prevent over-banking. Then, and only then, monitor the turn indicator. Very small adjustments of the bank angle are permissible, but this should hardly be necessary. Of course, at a slower airspeed—as, for example, in a holding pattern—the bank angle will have to be shallower to achieve the same rate of turn. It is a good idea to learn the right bank angle for one particular reduced airspeed that you might commonly employ. Finally, the roll-out should be brisk and coordinated, levelling the wings with aileron and rudder, then neutralizing the controls.

Turn indicators (or turn coordinators) may not all be perfectly accurate. It is a good idea to time some turns (e.g., exactly one minute for a 180-degree turn) in order to establish precisely where your own turn indicator should point for a standard rate turn.

Practice. We'll assume you are at 3000 feet and holding heading 165 when the practice exercise begins. Your check pilot plays the role of ATC and gives commands to turn to this or that heading. You acknowledge every time, and comply. The check pilot should score you according to your verbal responses, your ability to maintain headings precisely, your smoothness in turning to new headings, and your consistency in maintaining altitude.

> ATC: "2345 Juliet turn right heading 200 (two zero zero, not two hundred).
> You: "45 Juliet right to two zero zero." (And do it.)
> ATC: (A few minutes later): "45 Juliet left to 190."
> You: "45 Juliet left to 190." And do it. A 5 degree bank is enough.

Each time you roll out on a new heading, the check pilot should monitor the DG for a few minutes to see how well you are holding it. Heading deviation should never exceed 10 degrees, and as you improve your skill, you'll find it rarely exceeds 2 or 3 degrees.

> ATC (simulating a slip of the tongue): "45 Juliet right to 160."
>
> You (recognizing this doesn't make much sense—does he really want you to make a full circle?): "45 Juliet, is that RIGHT to 160?"
>
> ATC: "Negative, 45 Juliet, LEFT to 160. (Sometimes he might tell you he really meant it, for example to provide better separation from an aircraft just ahead of you. But don't be afraid to verify anything that seems odd.)

And so it goes. Your check pilot should go on inventing headings, some requiring only small changes, some being complete changes of course. Throughout the exercise the check pilot observes your altimeter, calling your attention to any changes as great as 50 feet. You, of course, if you're scanning well, will be correcting deviations when they are much smaller than that.

The check pilot should jot down the number of heading changes he calls out. For each deviation in heading greater than 10 degrees, you will score 10 points. For each case of overbanking (i.e., greater than standard rate turn), you'll score 10 points. For each altitude deviation greater than 50 feet you'll score 10 points, and 20 points additional for greater than 100 feet. For each failure to repeat back the heading, or to question a turn called out in the wrong direction, you'll score 10 points. Your final score will be the total number of points divided by the number of heading changes called out, i.e., it will be your average score per heading change. As in all these exercises, a score of zero wins the game. See Score Sheet, page 5-5.

Partial Panel.

Principles. In partial panel exercises we simulate the condition in which the main gyro instruments (DG and AI) are inoperative, as though your engine driven vacuum pump had failed; but you still have your electrically operated (in some aircraft Venturi operated) turn indicator. For partial panel work your check pilot will need some adhesive paper rectangles with which to cover up the DG and AI. Self-sticking removable labels (2 by 4 inch rectangles) obtainable at any stationery store work fine.

Without the DG, the only heading indicator you have is the magnetic compass. You'll remember that this instrument is useless in turns, and often useless during acceleration or deceleration. The only suitable way to make turns to headings, therefore, is by the method of timed turns. Your turn

Score Sheet: **Full Panel**

ITEM	1	2	3	4	5	6	7	8	9	10
Session:										
Date:										
Total number of heading changes.										
Heading deviation greater than 10°. (10 points)										
Overbanking in turn. (10 points)										
Altitude deviation greater than 50 ft. (10 points)										
---- greater than 100 ft. (20 additional)										
Failure to repeat heading or to question wrong command. (10 points)										
TOTAL POINT SCORE										
FINAL SCORE (= Total Point Score divided by number of heading changes.)										

indicator (needle or turn coordinator) is still working, since it is independently powered, so if you set up a standard rate turn (3 degrees per second) you can do pretty well in knowing when to roll out by dividing the number of degrees to be turned by 3 and turning that number of seconds. Thus, a 30 degree turn requires 10 seconds, and so on. Setting up the standard rate turn is a little more difficult without the AI because you can't establish the correct bank angle; you just have to use the turn indicator itself. After you roll out, you can check again on the magnetic compass, and make small corrections if they are needed.

The method of turning by the magnetic compass itself is amusing to practice and be able to do, but it is a messy procedure at best, and is really never necessary. Even if your clock stopped, you could count seconds well enough by the old "one one thousand, two one thousand, three one thousand" technique. Your chance of rolling out on the right heading will certainly be as good by this crude timed turn method as if you were trying to recall just which crazy things the compass does in turns to and from northerly headings, and which different crazy things it does in turns to and from southerly headings.

In partial panel work, your turn needle replaces the DG as your control instrument for wings-level flight, with the magnetic compass serving as monitoring instrument for maintaining the desired heading. How do you replace the pitch indicating function of the AI? Again, by using for both control and monitoring those instruments that were primarily monitoring instruments when the AI was functional. Thus, pitch is established by setting up the right cruise power setting and then the pitch trim that is required to give the proper cruise airspeed. Once the pitch is established by means of the ASI as control instrument, monitor the situation by means of the altimeter and VSI. If the airspeed is correct, then monitor the result. In changing pitch attitudes without the aid of the AI, remember that the aircraft's momentum causes a lag in airspeed change when the pitch is changed. This causes the only real problem in using the ASI as control instrument for a pitch change—the tendency to "chase the needle" unless you make pitch changes very cautiously and stop soon enough to anticipate the lag on the ASI.

This is a good place to discuss a more serious problem—loss of **all** your gyros in IFR conditions. The most important thing you need to do is fly wings level. The reason is that sooner or later your ship will dip a wing and you'll have no way to know it. As it rolls into a steeper bank, it will tend to nose down, picking up airspeed—the start of a "graveyard spiral". You don't know which way to roll out of the bank, but since your airspeed indicator tells you you're diving, you'll pull back on the yoke. This, of course, only tightens the spiral. So you MUST have a way of flying wings level. Here the magnetic compass is a lifesaver. If you're very skillful you can use it effectively on *any* heading, but if you fly a southerly heading it becomes a sure and sensitive wings-level indicator. As soon as the trouble begins, ease around to heading 180 (and tell ATC what you're doing). Now the slightest dropping of the left wing will show 179, 178, etc.; the slightest dropping of the right wing will show 181, 182, etc. Thus, you can make corrections promptly, before a significant bank develops. From there on, depend on ATC to help you out.

It's worth pointing out again that you have another wings-level indicator aboard if you have an ADF. This can be used on any heading, provided there is a good strong signal (radiobeacon or commercial broadcast station) directly ahead or behind. Again, as with the magnetic compass, dropping a wing and entering a turn will give you a needle deviation, which can be corrected promptly.

The ultimate in partial panel work is to assume that for some reason your altimeter has also malfunctioned. You then have to maintain altitude as best you can by means of the ASI. Working by "needle, ball, and airspeed" (in this exercise you are allowed your electrically driven turn indicator), you control pitch by maintaining the airspeed constant. You know already that with a constant power setting your indicated airspeed will reflect the pitch attitude. If the nose comes up, you will climb, and your airspeed will fall off. If the nose goes down, you will dive, and your airspeed will increase. So, if you hold the airspeed constant, you won't climb or dive, and it is surprising how constant your altitude will be.

Notice how valuable the vertical speed indicator (VSI) becomes in this exercise. It is a very sensitive trend instrument, which means that it tells you when your altitude **begins** to change, and you can make a tiny correction before the altimeter shows much deviation at all. Also, note that when the VSI needle starts to move and you respond with slight pressure or tension on the yoke, the instant the VSI needle stops is the moment you have returned to level flight, and at this instant the pressure or tension on the yoke should be removed. Otherwise, you will carry out a vertical S, porpoising rather than smoothly establishing level flight.

Finally, when you're pretty confident of your partial panel abilities under all the above conditions, cover up more and more instruments (including the MP gauge or tachometer) until you have **only** the needle (turn indicator), ball, and airspeed left. Then when you've mastered this too, cover the airspeed and see how well you can maintain a constant airspeed and constant altitude by the sound of the engine. Then cover the needle and try flying straight and level on a southerly heading, using the magnetic compass alone. To convince yourself of what happens when you have **no** means of levelling the wings, cover the magnetic compass too, and see how long you can fly before you enter a spiral dive—but have your check pilot ready to take over before things get out of hand.

Practice. When you have become expert in the full panel maneuvers, and your final score per session is no greater than 10 points, it is time to begin partial panel practice. The procedures for your check pilot calling out heading changes, for your acknowledging and complying, and for scoring are all exactly the same as with full panel exercises. At first, your scores will go up, because the task is intrinsically more difficult. But gradually, you will improve on this too, as your skill is sharpened by practice.

Start partial panel work by having the check pilot cover up the AI and DG, leaving everything else at your disposal, and practice straight flight (using the turn needle) and timed turns to headings. Make the simulation as realistic as possible by reporting to "ATC" every time an instrument "fails". Then uncover the AI and DG, and pretend your altimeter is inoperative by covering it up. Fly the various assigned headings, concentrating on maintaining cruise airspeed. Every few minutes the check pilot should uncover the altimeter momentarily, so you can see how well you're doing. The aim should be to stay within 200 feet of the assigned altitude for at least 5 minutes, and within 50 feet for any 1-minute period.

Continue modifying the instrument panel by covering up first one instrument, then another, and eventually having several covered simultaneously. You will find it challenging and interesting to see how well you can fly with a minimum of instrumentation. Eventually, with sufficient practice, your partial panel straight flight and turns to headings should score just as low as with full panel. You'll find now that your full-panel skills have improved greatly, and you'll wonder what was ever difficult about holding a course or turning to a new one and maintaining altitude with the AI and DG right in front of you.

Score Sheet: Partial Panel

ITEM	1	2	3	4	5	6	7	8	9	10
Session:										
Date:										
Total number of heading changes.										
Heading deviation greater than 10°. (10 points)										
Overbanking in turn. (10 points)										
Altitude deviation greater than 50 ft. (10 points)										
—— greater than 100 ft. (20 additional)										
Failure to repeat heading or to question wrong command. (10 points)										
TOTAL POINT SCORE										
FINAL SCORE (= Total Point Score divided by number of heading changes.)										

6. CLIMBS AND DESCENTS

Enroute Climbs and Descents.

    Principles. All climbs and descents are constant airspeed maneuvers. There are two kinds of climb: the **maximum performance climb**, either at best-rate airspeed or at best-angle airspeed; and the **cruise climb**, at an airspeed somewhere between best-rate and normal cruise, to obtain a moderate climb with good engine cooling and a satisfactory forward speed. There are also two kinds of descent: the **cruise descent**, at cruise airspeed with constant rate of descent, in small aircraft either 1000 feet per minute or 500 feet per minute; and the **approach descent**, inbound from a final approach fix, at a definite and constant reduced airspeed, in small aircraft commonly 80 knots.

    In IFR flight, with few exceptions, climbs are executed at the power setting and airspeed specified for best rate of climb in your aircraft. This might be, typically, with full throttle at 75 knots. For cruise climb the airspeed will be different, but the procedure is the same. First raise the nose to the appropriate pitch attitude on the AI, then watch the airspeed indicator as it falls off, and finally bring in climb power when the correct climb airspeed has been reached. Small pitch adjustments are made then, and elevator trim is adjusted to relieve control pressure. Levelling off from a climb is done in the same sequence. When the altimeter reaches the desired altitude, lower the nose to the appropriate pitch for level flight. This is called "stopping the altimeter", because you simply increase pressure on the yoke to whatever extent is needed to prevent any further gain in altitude, trimming out the pressure as the airspeed picks up. When the airspeed has returned to cruise—not before, unless the RPM is pushing redline—smoothly reduce power to the normal cruise setting. Then do whatever fine trimming is needed to let you fly level. According to the Airman's Information Manual, climbs and descents should be as fast as practicable until within 1000 feet of the assigned altitude, then at 500 feet per minute. In most small aircraft at gross you'd be lucky to climb as fast as 500 feet per minute. Rapid descents are possible but uncomfortable. Since the recommendation in the Airman's Information Manual is only that—not a regulation—I make a point of climbing and descending as nearly as possible at 500 feet per minute, except when a maximum performance climb is appropriate (e.g., a missed approach) or when a glide slope dictates a slower rate of descent. This is justified by the requirements of passenger comfort.

Cruise descents are simple. A certain reduced power setting (with a fixed-pitch prop this might typically be 2200 RPM) will give you a 500 ft/min descent if you just let the nose do what it wants to do, which is to drop slightly. The airspeed will remain close to its normal cruise value without any retrimming. Know the necessary power setting for your airplane; learn it through trial and error, then use it for every routine descent. A smooth transition from cruising level flight to a standard descent is accomplished as follows: Bring the power back briskly to the setting you know will be about right; let the nose drop, monitoring it on the AI and monitoring airspeed at the same time. Then when everything has settled down, monitor the rate of descent on the VSI. Don't forget to include the DG in your scan. Make fine elevator trim adjustments, if necessary, to keep the airspeed right where you want it. Remember that power controls the rate of climb or descent, while pitch controls the airspeed. So if the VSI doesn't show exactly 500 ft/min, make whatever fine power adjustments are necessary. Finally, when the altimeter shows the assigned altitude, bring in cruise power briskly, let the nose come back to cruise pitch on the AI, and make sure your heading hasn't wandered. Cruise descents are easy because the airspeed never changes and virtually no retrimming is required. The very same procedure (with a different power setting) would apply to any other rate of descent at cruise airspeed.

Practice. Now that you can hold a heading without trouble, climbs and descents should be easy. Have your check pilot call out various climb and descent commands for you to execute, maintaining an assigned heading all the while. You will be describing a sort of vertical S in a straight line—first up 500 feet, then level, then down 500, level again, up 1000, level, down 500, level, and so on. Let's suppose you're starting the exercise at 3000 feet in level flight on a heading of 180.

> Check Pilot: "2345 Juliet climb and maintain 3500 (three thousand five hundred)."
> You: "45 Juliet climb and maintain three thousand five hundred—and we're leaving three thousand."

(Note that you first acknowledge the clearance by repeating it back, and then you comply with the requirement to report leaving an assigned altitude. Some clearances might require you to accept and repeat back, but not initiate the climb immediately.)

So now you do it. As you pull back on the yoke, scan the AI and the DG, setting up the right pitch on the AI (usually 2-3 bar-widths high) and watching to be sure you don't wander from your 180 degree heading on the DG. Then let your scan include the airspeed indicator, and when the climb airspeed is right, bring in the power. Back to the DG while you're trimming. Then bring the altimeter into your scan. When it shows 3500, nose down to level flight pitch on the AI, and check the heading again as your eyes scan over to the airspeed indicator and altimeter. It takes more and more forward pressure to stop the altimeter as the airspeed builds up, so start trimming it out. When you become skilled in this maneuver, the altimeter will really **stop**, not exceeding the assigned altitude by even 10 feet. Finally, as the airspeed reaches cruise, bring back the power, check the heading again, and trim to perfection.

You: "45 Juliet level at three thousand five hundred."

(Not required by regulations, but do it every time. It helps the controller—so it helps you—if he knows when you get to the assigned altitude.)

Check Pilot: "2345 Juliet descend and maintain two thousand five hundred."

You: "45 Juliet descend and maintain two thousand five hundred—and we're leaving three thousand five hundred now." (And do it.)

A typical problem you may encounter in descents is a reluctance on your part to allow the nose-low pitch that is required to maintain airspeed. For some curious psychological reason, you will have a tendency to pull back the yoke to keep things level on the AI, and this defeats you in two ways. First, your airspeed falls off to no purpose, confusing the controller, who is figuring out how to sequence you with other IFR traffic. Second, the higher angle of attack generates more lift, so that your rate of descent is much less than you want it to be. Solve this problem by paying close attention to the airspeed indicator, and repeating over and over: "Yoke controls airspeed."

After you are doing a pretty good job with straight climbs and descents, introduce heading changes into the picture. At first, you will find, everything goes to pieces. If the headings are right, the altitudes are wrong; if you level out at the right altitude, you find you've forgotten to stop your turn. But with practice, everything will settle down, and you'll experience the real satisfaction of handling any combination of climbs, descents, and turns to headings.

Your check pilot should try to do what a good instructor would do—take you a step at a time, without overwhelming you, but always pushing you a little farther. The trick is to start out giving you one command at a time, in such a way that you can complete one operation before having to complete the other. For instance, while you are flying straight and level on heading 180 at 3000, the command to climb and maintain 4000 is given. Then, only when you are into the climb and things are, for the moment, settled down, he should command a small turn, for example, right to 200. This turn can be completed before you have to do anything about the climb, which is taking care of itself pretty well. Then, on heading 200, your altimeter will approach 4000, and you can go through the level-off procedure. But as you get better, he should make it harder, for instance by ordering a 360 to the right. This turn will take 2 minutes, so the rollout from the turn will come just about at the same time as you reach 4000 and have to level off. Eventually, your check pilot will learn how to make the challenges as difficult as a good instructor can—by devilishly timing the turn commands to coincide with the most difficult parts of the climbs or descents. He should also give you some practice in starting climbs or descents simultaneously with turns to headings—all in one command, e.g., 2345 Juliet turn left heading 030, descend and maintain 2000.

Scoring on enroute climbs and descents will follow the usual system, with specific errors assigned point values, and the aim being to minimize the score. Each deviation of more than 5 knots from the appropriate airspeed during a climb or descent merits 10 points, and deviations greater than 10 knots score 20 points additional. Passing the assigned altitude for level-off by more than 50 feet earns 10 points, with an additional 20 for altitude error of more than 100 feet; these apply both in levelling off and during level flight portions of the exercise. Deviating more than 10 degrees from the assigned heading gets 10 points, with an additional 20 for deviating more than 20 degrees. Failure to repeat back a clearance (i.e., any climb, descent, or turn instruction) has a 10 point penalty, as does failing to report leaving or reaching an assigned altitude. As with previous scoring, a total point score is obtained by averaging—dividing the total number of points by the number of climbs plus the number of descents. A score of zero wins the game, but expect pretty big scores for a while; you'll have room for improvement. See Score Sheet, page 6-5.

Descents at Approach Airspeed.

Principles. Approach descents are carried out at reduced airspeed—whatever is appropriate for your ship. We'll assume 80 knots, a typical approach speed for a small aircraft. The principle is the same, however, whether the chosen speed is 60, 80, or 100 knots. (These particular speeds are useful because they correspond exactly to those given in the "time to missed approach" tables at the bottom of the approach plates.) A typical approach on a glide slope is at a vertical speed of approximately 400 ft/min—approximately, because it depends not only on your airspeed, but also on your headwind or tailwind. Don't worry about it. On the glide slope, you'll maintain the approach airspeed; and you'll stay on the glide slope by adjusting the power—whatever it takes. Too low—more power; too high—less power. On nonprecision approaches, you'll want to get down to minimums as soon as you reasonably can, but you certainly don't want

Score Sheet: Enroute Climbs and Descents.

ITEM	1	2	3	4	5	6	7	8	9	10
Session:										
Date:										
Total number of climbs plus descents.										
Airspeed deviation greater than 5 knots. (10 points)										
—— greater than 10 knots. (20 additional)										
Altitude deviation in level flight or level-off greater than 50 ft. (10 points)										
—— greater than 100 ft. (20 additional)										
Heading deviation greater than 10°. (10 points)										
—— greater than 20°. (20 additional)										
Failure to repeat clearance. (10 points)										
Failure to report leaving or reaching an assigned altitude. (10 points)										
TOTAL POINT SCORE										
FINAL SCORE (= Total Point Score divided by number of climbs and descents.)										

an excessive rate of descent, so you'll just choose a 500 ft/min descent at approach airspeed, using whatever power you need to keep the VSI needle right on 500.

The transition from cruise to approach speed is normally carried out at the final approach fix—the outer marker on ILS and localizer approaches. If the glide slope is intercepted before reaching the outer marker (the usual state of affairs in ILS approaches), the transition should be accomplished then. First, reduce the power to a setting well below what you know will be needed. Then, trade off airspeed for altitude, i.e., trim nose up, as you start your descent on the glide slope, while the airspeed falls to the desired value. Then, say at 80 knots, smartly bring the power up to the required setting.

Practice. When you have mastered climbs and cruise descents, and your total scores are showing a healthy trend downward, start practicing descents at reduced (approach) airspeed. It might go something like this. You're at 5000 MSL, with terrain at 2000 MSL, and your heading is 180. For this exercise we place an imaginary airport at a safe altitude, say 3500 MSL. During the "approach", you'll concentrate on holding the heading (here 180) very exactly. Even the missed approach procedure will be a straight-out climb on a heading of 180.

> Check Pilot: "2345 Juliet at the outer marker, cleared for the approach."
> You: "45 Juliet at the outer, cleared for the approach."

Start timing at the final approach fix; this should become automatic. If you have a stopwatch, start it. If not, note the time on your panel clock. In either case, write down in bold, clear, legible numbers what the time will be at the missed approach point. This is given on the approach plates; it is usually between 2 and 7 minutes. In this exercise, invent some elapsed time (e.g., 3 minutes 35 seconds), long enough so you can expect to reach minimums before the time expires.

At the same time and without delay (you'll wonder how you can be expected to do everything at once, but you'll learn how, with practice) reduce power below what you know you'll need eventually, and maintain altitude by gradually raising the nose, letting the airspeed fall off to 80 knots (or 100, or whatever you decide you like). During this airspeed reduction, the altimeter should not have moved at all. Now setting the pitch where you think it should be on the AI (probably one bar low), bring in power gradually, to give you a 500 ft/min descent. Retrim for the lower airspeed. The first part of this maneuver—the airspeed reduction—is new, but the rest is basically the same as you've done many times before. The only difference is that with your greater angle of attack (more lift) your power setting will have to be lower than in a cruise descent—1700 or 1800 RPM would be typical.

Since the airport is assumed to be at 3500 MSL, your minimum descent altitude (MDA) for the nonprecision approach will most likely be around 4000, although this will vary greatly from airport to airport. With full ILS, your decision height (DH) will usually be 200 feet above the airport. So assume some minimum before you start the maneuver, and practice the missed approach procedure. First, you must never under any circumstances descend below the designated minimum (not even 10 feet below!) unless you can see the runway threshold (or associated markings or approach lights) and are in a position for a normal landing. This means stopping the altimeter sharply and completely at the minimum altitude, just as you practiced in cruise descents. Second, when the missed approach point (such as a middle marker) is reached or the specified time from the final approach fix has elapsed, and the airport is not in sight, you must initiate the missed approach at once. This means, without a moment's delay or hesitation— "immediately" (in ATC terminology)—starting a maximum performance climb. Reading accident reports will convince you of the wisdom of these two absolute rules on approaches. Once you accept the notion of descending "a little" below minimums in the hope of breaking out of the clouds, or the notion that you might see the runway if you go a few seconds beyond the permissible elapsed time, you are headed for disaster sooner or later. When you reach the missed approach point or the time elapses, and you don't see the runway or approach lights, add immediate climb power, raise the nose to the appropriate pitch angle on the AI, and clean up the airplane (gear and flaps).

To help you learn how to execute a missed approach promptly, without hesitation, your check pilot should sometimes call out "missed approach" unexpectedly during your approach descent. At other times he should let you initiate your own missed approaches at predetermined altitudes. At first, do your simulated missed approaches straight ahead, maintaining the approach heading, as described here. Later, as you get better at it, have your check pilot invent some turn to a new heading as part of the missed approach procedure, so you can practice the abrupt climb and the turn simultaneously.

Scoring for approach descents is the same as for cruise descents, as far as airspeed and heading are concerned, but you get 50 points if you ever descend below minimums. You score 50 points for failing to recognize the elapsed time at which the missed approach is to be initiated. In the missed approach phase, you score 10 points for deviation greater than 5 knots from best-rate airspeed. Divide the total points by the number of descents attempted, to get an average final score. When you make a zero score, you're ready to try simulated approaches with actual approach plates. But first, you'll have to learn precision tracking of VOR radials, to which the next chapter is devoted.

Score Sheet: Descents at Approach Airspeed.

ITEM	1	2	3	4	5	6	7	8	9	10
Session:										
Date:										
Total number of descents at approach airspeed										
Airspeed deviation greater than 5 knots (10 points)										
—— greater than 10 knots. (20 additional)										
Vertical speed deviation greater than 50 ft/min. (10 points)										
—— greater than 100 ft/min. (20 additional)										
Heading deviation greater than 10°. (10 points)										
—— greater than 20°. (20 additional)										
Failure to repeat clearance. (10 points)										
Descent below minimums. (50 points)										
Exceeding allowed elapsed time. (50 points)										
Sloppy initiating of missed approach. (20 points)										
TOTAL POINT SCORE										
FINAL SCORE (= Total Point Score divided by number of descents.)										

7. VOR TRACKING AND VOR APPROACHES

Enroute Tracking.

Principles. Since the airways usually run in straight lines between VOR stations, and since many IFR approaches are based on VOR stations, a key skill in IFR flying is the ability to track radials accurately and without great effort. It has to become second nature to you, so you can devote your attention simultaneously to the various other tasks that make for a safe cruising flight or a safe approach.

Flying outbound from a VOR is easiest because the farther you go from the station, the more widely separated are the radials, which fan outward in all directions from the VOR. Near the VOR the distance from the 240 radial to the 241 radial (for example) may be only a few feet, but at a distance of 30 miles it is half a mile. Thus, if you start outbound from the VOR with your OBS set to the radial you want to track, and the omni needle is slightly off center, you have plenty of time to try out different heading corrections until the needle finally centers. But, as you'll discover, things have to be done much faster flying inbound because as you get closer to the VOR, the needle will move much more quickly away from the center position unless you pin down the crab correction faster. In a surprisingly short time the needle can move full scale and be "pinned to the peg".

To track a radial outbound, you first have to intercept it. Usually 30 degrees is a good intercept angle, but depending upon how far you are from the radial, you may want to choose a much larger angle or a smaller one (as small as a few degrees). It's just a matter of simple common sense. You don't want to spend all day intercepting the radial, but then neither do you want to fly right past it and then have to intercept again from the other side.

Fig. 7-1 gives the procedure, step by step. Suppose you want to intercept and track outbound the 080 radial, and that your position is somewhat to the right, perhaps on the 100 radial, as in (1). Set up the radial you want on the OBS, and turn to that heading. The indicator will show FROM, and you will be flying approximately parallel to the course you have chosen. The needle will then show you the position of that radial; in this example, the needle will point to the left. Now, as in (2), turn toward the needle by an amount you think should be a good intercept angle, say 30 degrees. Now your heading will be 050 and you should be flying toward the chosen radial. Hold your heading exactly, and see if the needle moves toward the center. If there is no movement at all in about 30 seconds, increase your intercept angle, i.e., turn further left to a new heading, perhaps to 040. Again wait, then again change heading if necessary. Of course, you won't exceed a 90 degree intercept angle, because that would have you flying back toward the station.

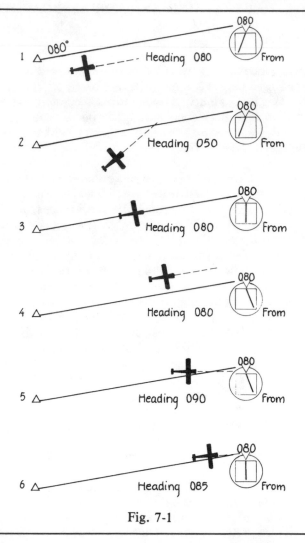

Fig. 7-1

Let's suppose the needle starts to move after your first heading change. Watch its rate of movement closely. The whole point is to intercept the radial smoothly. You don't want to overshoot and then make an abrupt turn with excessive banking to get back on the radial again. So, as the needle moves toward the center, begin your turn toward the heading you'll eventually want, i.e., the course of the radial, in this case 080 degrees. This should bring you to the situation depicted in (3), where you are on course, your heading is 080, and the needle is centered.

As soon as you detect a slight but definite movement of the needle in either direction, make a small heading correction toward the needle. In (4), a right crosswind has evidently drifted you to the left. Your heading is still 080, but the needle shows you that your chosen course is now to your right. In (5) you have made a 10 degree correction toward the needle, so your heading is now 090. Soon, as in (6), the needle will center again. Since heading 090 would now take you across to the other side of the course, as soon as the needle centers, you take out half of your correction. Now your heading is 085, probably just right to compensate for the crosswind, and the needle stays centered.

If you do a good job of holding your headings, and if your DG hasn't precessed, the only cause of needle deviation will be wind drift. Information gained in this way about the prevailing wind will be useful to you in flying holding patterns, as described in the next chapter. When you make heading corrections, how large should they be? That depends on how far you are from the VOR; the farther away you are, the larger the corrections can be to compensate for a given amount of needle deviation. The needle measures only the angular distance off course, and a given angular distance means a greater actual distance, the farther you are from the station. With a DME this problem becomes very simple; just make your initial heading corrections in degrees equal to your distance in miles from the station. If you know or can guess the distance, you can apply the same rule even without a DME. Otherwise, use trial and error. If a 20 degree correction starts the needle moving back to the center too quickly, take out half the correction, and if 10 degrees is still too much, make it 5 degrees. The important principle is to make your corrections promptly and frequently. Don't wait until the needle is nearly up against the peg. The initial aim is to stop the needle wherever it is on the scale, i.e., to put an end to the drifting tendency. **Note the heading at which this happens**, for this will be the heading you'll want to fly finally, after you're on course again. Then correct a little more, to center the needle. Finally, with the needle centered, go back to the heading you noted, where there was no needle movement.

The key to this whole exercise is your ability to fly an absolutely constant heading, and for this your DG is the primary control instrument. The omni needle is your monitoring instrument; it tells you if your constant heading is correct or not. Don't "chase the needle", i.e., don't become impatient and make larger and larger heading changes toward the needle, or before you realize what is happening, the needle will swing past the center and you'll be chasing it on the other side. You might get away with rough technique flying outbound, but it will never work flying inbound, when ever smaller and more delicate heading changes are needed as you approach the VOR.

What's new in this exercise is that you have to include the omni needle in your scan. Very likely, you'll be so busy at first trying to keep it centered that you'll concentrate on heading to the detriment of altitude. The trick is to include more and more instruments in your scan, without neglecting any one. Just as you did before the VOR tracking problem complicated matters, you must pay especial attention to correcting altitude deviations while they are small, using prompt but very slight yoke pressure.

When you are well established on the radial, flying outbound, make a standard rate turn and intercept the same radial inbound. IFR students have a lot of trouble with the concept of tracking a radial inbound, because they forget that the course will be the reciprocal of the radial. Thus, tracking the 080 radial inbound means flying a course of 260 degrees. The OBS must be set for 260, and the indicator will show TO. In all VOR navigation, the OBS setting must correspond approximately with your heading, as shown on the DG, whether you are flying to the station (the indicator will show TO) or from the station (the indicator will show FROM). If this rule is followed without exception, you will always make corrections by flying toward the needle. The only time this principle is not operative is in flying the back course of a localizer, where you have no choice but to fly with "reverse sensing", i.e., to make corrections away from the needle.

Tracking inbound, you'll notice as you get closer to the VOR how much more sensitive the needle becomes. Your headings will have to be held with perfect accuracy, and your heading corrections will become smaller and smaller—10 degrees, then 5 degrees, then 2 degrees, eventually even 1 degree. Refuse to accept a needle that's off center. Make a tiny heading change, then wait just long enough (5-10 seconds when you're very close to the VOR) to see if that did the trick. If not, make another tiny change. The aim in inbound tracking is to cross the VOR with the needle absolutely centered. At the very last moment, as you cross the "cone of confusion" right over the station, you'll recognize the sudden erratic swings of the needle. Don't try to chase it. Just hold your last heading until the indicator flips from TO to FROM.

When you cross a VOR, the rule is TIME, TURN, TALK, in that order. Note the time, start the turn to your outbound heading, and then—and only when the airplane is well in hand—report to ATC. When you turned inbound after tracking a radial outbound, you reset your OBS to correspond with the course you wanted to fly. Remember to do the same now. As you start your turn, set the OBS to the outbound radial you want to intercept.

Practice. Find a VOR (let's call it MYSTIC) where you can safely exercise a few thousand feet above. Pick a definite altitude (e.g., 4000 ft) and hold it exactly. Trim the airplane and set the power at a comfortable cruise setting. Now rotate the OBS until the needle centers with the indicator showing FROM. This tells you what radial you are on.

Now your check pilot should call out a command to intercept a nearby radial. Suppose your OBS shows 153. He might say: "2345 Juliet intercept and track outbound the MYSTIC 160 radial."

You acknowledge: "45 Juliet outbound the MYSTIC 160," and immediately start a turn to 160. While you are turning, set up 160 on your OBS. Since you were on the 153 radial, the 160 radial is to your right, and the needle will now point to the right. Therefore, don't roll out of your turn at 160, but rather at an intercept heading such as 170, 180, 190 or even greater, depending upon the circumstances. Then you follow the interception procedures already described.

Once you are established outbound, your check pilot should observe you for about 3 minutes, especially rating your ability to keep the needle centered and hold altitude at the same time. Then he should unexpectedly call out a command to turn and intercept the same or a different radial inbound. For example: "2345 Juliet turn left, intercept and track inbound the 140 radial."

It's going to take you a full minute to turn back toward the VOR, so start doing it immediately. Students are often uncertain about exactly what they are going to do, and consequently do nothing. It's worse to go blundering off into the boondocks after ATC tells you to go somewhere else than it is to start complying promptly even if you haven't got it all worked out in your head. So in this case start the standard rate left turn as soon as you acknowledge. Also during the turn remember to reset your OBS to the reciprocal of the radial you want to track inbound, in this case to 320. By the time your heading is coming around toward 320, your needle will be giving you good guidance for the intercept.

Now you continue all the way to the VOR, pretending, if you like, that this is a VOR approach, with the VOR right on the field. If your needle isn't centered as you cross the VOR, your chance of completing the approach safely is very poor. Before you reach the VOR, your check pilot should call out a new radial to track outbound. Then as you cross the VOR, you note the time, start your turn, and report: "45 Juliet at MYSTIC, 13, 4000, turning to 180 (or whatever)". (Here 13—say "one three"—is the time, in minutes past the hour, when you crossed the VOR).

Your check pilot should, of course, use the actual name of the VOR you are using, whatever it is. Besides calling out commands, what should your check pilot be watching for as you struggle along?

(1) Traffic. This is his number one job. A lot of traffic tends to converge at a VOR, so the check pilot should keep his neck craning all the time. There should be a clear understanding between you that he may take the controls at any time (and you will instantly relinquish them) to avoid a potential collision hazard.

(2) Terrain. It would be pretty foolish to let you fly into a hillside. If there's any chance of that, go to a higher altitude.

(3) Your performance. Since you will be concentrating on maintaining heading, he should pay especial attention to your altitude control, calling your attention to deviations of 50 feet. When things go poorly in a new exercise, there's usually a simple reason: tension. The check pilot can pick this up by just looking at your left hand. If it's gripping the yoke tightly and your knuckles are white, the situation should be called to your attention. Relax. Let the airplane fly itself; just guide it along, holding the yoke very lightly between your thumb and first two fingers. Then if things won't settle down even after you've relaxed, the ship is probably out of trim. Trim it carefully, and you'll free more of your energy for the VOR tracking task.

Your check pilot should keep score as follows: 10 points for each altitude deviation of 50 feet, and an additional 20 points for 100 foot deviation; 10 points each time the needle hits the peg during inbound tracking (not counting the abrupt swing-out at station passage), and 20 points during outbound tracking; 20 points for each failure to reset the OBS on station passage or when turning inbound after outbound tracking; 10 points for each failure to report station passage correctly (Position, Time, Altitude, and What you're doing next); 20 points for forgetting to report station passage at all; 10 points for repeating a clearance incorrectly or failing to repeat it at all. The total point score accumulated is divided by the number of outbound trackings plus the number of inbound trackings, to obtain a final average score.

A half hour of this exercise at a time will probably be enough, especially in the early sessions. You should see some real improvement before you start fatiguing. As your skill improves, this whole exercise becomes easier, and you'll wonder what was ever so hard about it.

Time to Station.

Principles. There are several acceptable ways to determine your distance and/or time to VOR without a DME. All of them depend on timing how long it takes to travel a certain angular distance, i.e., from one given radial to another. An elementary example of such a procedure—although not a

Score Sheet: Enroute Tracking.

Session:	1	2	3	4	5	6	7	8	9	10
Date:										
ITEM Total number of outbound trackings plus inbound trackings.										
Altitude deviation greater than 50 ft. (10 points)										
—— greater than 100 ft. (20 additional)										
Pegging the needle during inbound tracking. (10 points)										
—— during outbound tracking. (20 points)										
Failure to reset OBS on station passage or turning inbound. (20 points)										
Failure to report station passage correctly. (10 points)										
Forgetting to report station passage. (20 points)										
Repeating a clearance incorrectly or failure to repeat at all. (10 points)										
TOTAL POINT SCORE										
FINAL SCORE (= Total Point Score divided by total number of outbound plus inbound trackings.)										

practical one—would be to fly one leg of an equilateral triangle with the VOR as its apex. As shown in Fig. 7-2, if you flew from whichever radial you were on to a radial 60 degrees away, and if you made an angle of 60 degrees with the radial you started from, it would take you just as long to get to the new radial as it would later take to get from there to the VOR. In all these problems the no-wind condition is assumed.

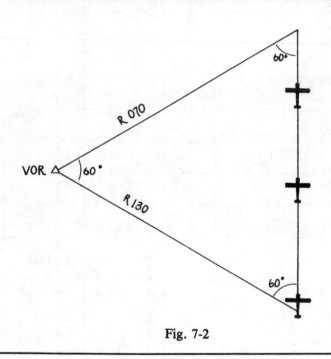

Fig. 7-2

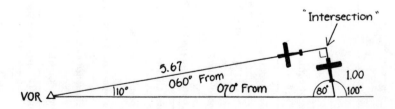

Fig. 7-3

The procedure shown in the diagram would be foolish because you would end up flying twice as long and twice as far as if you had flown directly to the VOR in the first place. But by applying simple trigonometry a reasonable procedure can be followed. A right triangle containing a 10 degree angle and an 80 degree angle has its perpendicular sides in the ratio 5.67 to 1. (See Fig. 7-3). To reduce the procedure to a handy and simple one that doesn't require trigonometric tables or computer work, this ratio is called 6 to 1. Therefore, as the diagram shows, if you turn 80 degrees from the radial you're on, and fly to a radial that is 10 degrees away, that flight will take you one-sixth as long as the subsequent flight to the VOR.

Practice. Here is the actual procedure:

1. Determine what radial you are on in the usual way by centering the needle with the indicator in the FROM position.

2. Turn to a heading 100 degrees greater or less than the bearing of the radial, whichever is the shortest turn to the new heading.

3. As you roll out on the new heading, center the needle again, quite exactly. Then rotate the OBS exactly 10 degrees in the direction that will cause the needle to point toward the station, i.e., left if the VOR is to your left, right if it is to your right.

4. Start timing the moment you set the OBS. You are now set up as for any intersection. The needle points toward the station until you reach the intersection, then centers at the intersection. The "intersection" in this case is the point where your course crosses the radial that is 10 degrees distant from the radial you started on. Continue timing until the needle centers again, concentrating all the while on holding your heading, by focusing on the index of the AI, and monitoring the DG.

5. Note the elapsed time in **seconds**, and also note the actual time on your clock in minutes past the hour.

6. Before you do any calculating, the moment you complete the timing, rotate the OBS until the needle centers again with the indicator showing TO, and turn to fly directly inbound to the VOR.

7. Divide the elapsed time (in seconds) by 10, to get the time in **minutes** to the station. This simple rule results from multiplying the elapsed time in seconds times 6, as described earlier, and then dividing by 60 to get an answer in minutes: seconds X 6 ÷ 60 = seconds ÷ 10. Add the estimate of time-to-station to the actual time you noted in step 5, to obtain an estimated time of arrival at the station.

Knowing your airspeed, you could, of course, compute the approximate **distance** to the station, but this is virtually never required; it is principally useful for lost VFR pilots who are trying to locate themselves on the sectional chart. Even the **time**-to-station estimate is rarely needed in these days of radar, airways, intersections, and DME. But occasionally the technique may be useful; it provides a method of telling ATC when you'll be at a VOR, and thus it allows the controller to coordinate your movements and clearances with those of other aircraft in order to provide adequate separation.

The real fun of this exercise—and the reward—is to continue your inbound flight all the way to the VOR, once you've computed your ETA, and see how accurately it works out. Small discrepancies are to be expected because of unknown wind effects, which you couldn't take into account, but an error of more than 10% probably means you did something wrong. Crossing the VOR right on your ETA will give you a foretaste of the satisfaction you'll gain later from successful enroute estimates and approaches under simulated or actual IFR conditions.

Your check pilot should unexpectedly ask you for a time-to-station estimate from time to time, when you are 5-10 miles from a VOR. He should monitor the procedure, scoring 10 points for each of the following errors: failure to set the OBS to the radial you are on, with the needle centered and the indicator showing FROM; failure to add or subtract 100 correctly and to assume the correct heading perpendicular to the radial toward which you must fly; failure to hold the heading perfectly; failure to center the needle again when you are on the correct heading; failure to time correctly; failure to note the actual clock time and to derive a correct ETA. Altitude deviations are scored as in the previous exercises: 10 points for a deviation greater than 50 feet, 20 points additional for a deviation greater than 100 feet. The final average score is the total point score divided by the number of trials in the session. See Score Sheet, page 7-11.

Simulated VOR Approaches.

Principles. A VOR approach combines what you have learned to do already—a descent at constant heading and reduced airspeed, and tracking inbound to a VOR or outbound from a VOR. There are basically two kinds of VOR approach. In one the VOR is a final approach fix, and you let down on a definite radial to the specified minimum descent altitude (MDA) while timing to the missed approach point (MAP). In the other, the VOR is on the field, and you let down from the final approach fix (an intersection, usually, or a DME fix) while tracking inbound on a specified radial. When the VOR is on the field, it is the MAP and no timing is necessary. If the field has an ILS and you have no glide slope receiver, you can fly a localizer (LOC) approach, which is the same as an approach to a VOR on the field, with two differences.

Score Sheet: Time to Station.

ITEM	1	2	3	4	5	6	7	8	9	10
Session:										
Date:										
Total number of trials.										
Failure to set the OBS to the radial with indicator in FROM position and needle centered. (10 points)										
Failure to add or subtract 100 correctly and assume correct heading. (10 points)										
Failure to hold heading perfectly. (10 points)										
Failure to center needle again on correct heading. (10 points)										
Failure to time correctly. (10 points)										
Failure to note actual clock time and compute a correct ETA. (10 points)										
Altitude deviation greater than 50 ft. (10 points)										
——— greater than 100 ft. (20 additional)										
TOTAL POINT SCORE										
FINAL SCORE (= Total Point Score divided by total number of trials.)										

First, rotating the OBS has no effect on the needle, since it is automatically tuned to the localizer approach course; nevertheless, it is good practice to set the OBS to the inbound course to remind you constantly of what your heading should be in the no-wind condition. Second, the needle is four times more sensitive than with a VOR; full needle deflection is 2.5 degrees instead of 10 degrees off course. Thus, although it is certainly more demanding to fly a localizer approach than a VOR approach, it is also a great deal safer, and consequently your MDA is usually correspondingly lower.

Certain things have to be done routinely at the final approach fix as you start your final approach. (1) Landing checklist, whatever it calls for in your aircraft. (2) Start timing. (3) Reduce your airspeed to the definite final approach speed you use, usually 80 knots or 100 knots. (4) Start your descent, and descend as rapidly as practicable to the MDA. It is important to get to the MDA as soon as possible so that you will have a good chance to break out of the clouds in ample time to get set up for landing, rather than barely breaking out only seconds before the MAP. (5) Simultaneously with the above—but remember to fly the airplane first and talk later—report the final approach fix inbound, usually to the tower or a flight service station on the field, but in the absence of both, to Approach Control or Center, as instructed.

During the approach, and until you either have the airport in sight or execute a missed approach, there are five critical things to monitor by constant scanning: (1) Your airspeed, which should be absolutely constant, with trim doing all the work for you. (2) Your heading, which should not deviate by even one degree from the chosen value. (3) The needle, which should remain perfectly centered throughout the approach. (4) The altimeter, which must never, under any conditions, be allowed to go below the MDA—not even 10 feet below. (5) The VSI, which you control with the throttle, and which will help you make a smooth descent to the MDA in good time. You should know from previous study of the approach plate just what vertical speed will do the job for you; you get this from the distance shown on the profile view from the final approach fix to the MAP, and your known approach airspeed.

You will read much argument about whether to control your descent (especially on a glide slope) with elevator and your airspeed with throttle, or whether elevator controls airspeed and throttle controls the rate of descent. If you have followed the principles expounded by Langewiesche, as insisted on throughout this book, you will realize the foolishness of changing all the procedures now, in the most delicate maneuver you have to master. To recapitulate briefly, an airplane is trimmed pretty closely to maintain a **given airspeed**, and that is exactly what you want to maintain on final approach. At that airspeed, if you are descending too fast (for example), and pull up with elevator, you will momentarily gain some lift and slow your descent, but then—unless you advance the power—you will descend even faster than before. So in this method you can probably perform a vertical S above and below a certain glide slope, but you'll be juggling both yoke and throttle— a poor way to make a smooth approach. By trimming for the desired airspeed, you can virtually fly with your hands off the yoke, making small power changes as needed with the throttle. Since you don't need to push and pull on the yoke, you can even use a couple of fingers to maintain wings level, if needed, while you make small (very small) heading changes with rudder. This makes for a very smooth heading hold through a series of tiny skids. Many pilots find this easier than trying to make very tiny banks with aileron, since overbanking is a common tendency.

The technique of the missed approach was discussed and practiced in the last chapter. It is the most important part of an approach. It has to be executed promptly and correctly at the MAP. You must firmly resist the desire to sneak a little lower if you can't see the runway or the approach lights, even if you catch glimpses of the ground under you. You don't really know what's ahead, and if you bust the minimums, you are giving away the elaborate protection that FAA arranged for you when they set the MDA for each particular airport and each particular type of approach at that airport. If you don't believe it, read the accident reports compiled by the Civil Aeronautics Board, for IFR approach accidents. "Descended below minimums" is the sad and repetitive conclusion.

When you reach the MAP, you are already at or very near your best rate of climb speed. Add climb power and raise the nose to what you know is the right pitch attitude, clean up the airplane if necessary and carry out the missed approach procedure just as it is specified on the approach plate. You should have studied it, and your COM and NAV radios should be set up for it in advance, if possible.

Practice. You'll need a nearby VOR, one without too much converging traffic, and not, of course, in a TCA. Don't worry if it's on the airport; you'll be more than 3000 feet above it, well out of the airport traffic area. The idea is to pretend that this particular VOR is some other one, **for which you have the approach plate.** You only have to change all the altitudes on the approach plate by some fixed number of thousands of feet—or you may not have to change them at all. Start with an approach in which the VOR is the final approach fix, and the approach consists of a letdown for a certain number of minutes on a certain radial toward the airport. The procedure is best understood by a specific example. Fig. 7-4 is the Jeppesen Approach Plate for the VOR Rwy 11 approach at Prescott, Arizona. The airport elevation is seen to be 5042'. We'll practice this approach using as our actual VOR the one on the field at San Jose, California (elevation 56'). Since we want to be at least 3000' above the San Jose airport, but not a great deal higher, we'll **subtract 2000 feet from all altitudes** shown on the Prescott plate. Thus, the simulated air-

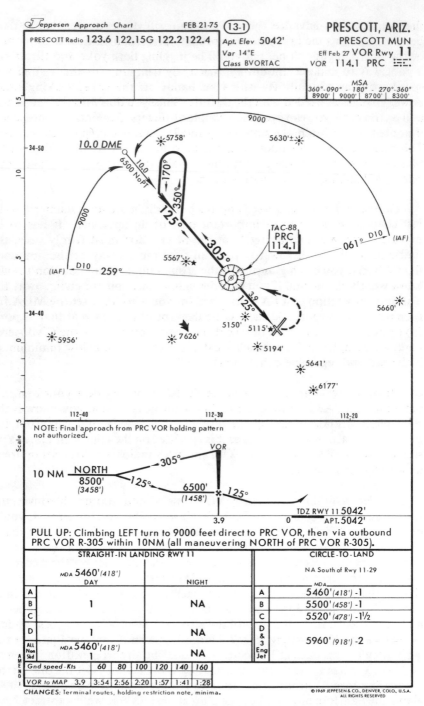

Fig. 7-4

port elevation becomes 3042', and the altitude approaching the VOR for a straight-in approach will be 6500' — 2000' = 4500'. You can first practice the direct approach inbound on the 305 radial with no procedure turn. Crossing the simulated PRC VOR (actually San Jose, 114.1, SJC) inbound at 4500', you reduce speed to 80 knots, note the time, and start your descent on a course of 125°. For a straight-in landing your MDA is 3460', and your missed approach point is reached 2 minutes and 56 seconds after leaving the VOR. You probably don't yet subscribe to the Jeppesen or NOS Approach Plates, but for the purposes of these exercises you can collect more than you'll ever be able to use by asking a friend who has them to give you all his discards. Since many replacement plates are issued each week, with small changes in procedures or radio frequencies, one throws away hundreds of these approach plates each year.

Next try approaches in which the VOR is on the field. An example, in Fig. 7-5, is the VOR Rwy 16 approach at Everett, Washington. Here the field elevation is 603', so **add 3000' to all altitudes** shown. Then the simulated airport elevation is 3603', the transition altitude crossing the VOR outbound (high passage) is 1800' + 3000' = 4800', and the descent to minimums begins when the inbound course (the 340 radial) is intercepted. Straight-in MDA is 4020'. Since the VOR itself is the missed approach point, there is nothing to time during the approach.

In these simulated approaches, since you'll never have the runway of intended landing in sight (it's not there!) you'll have good practice in missed approach procedures. Execute these exactly as specified on the plates. In the Prescott approach, when your time elapses, set up a maximum performance climb, start a left turn (standard rate—be careful!), climb to 7000' (= 9000' — 2000') direct to the VOR, then outbound on the 305 radial. This sets you up for another procedure turn and another try at the approach. In the Everett approach, when you cross the VOR inbound, start a climbing left turn to 5000' (= 2000' + 3000') proceeding outbound on the 275 radial. After reaching 5000' return to the VOR and hold northwest in the pattern shown (see Chapter 8).

A great advantage of these simulated approaches with real plates is that you will become familiar with a great many different approaches—and each approach has its own distinctive features. At the same time, you can avoid cluttering the real approaches in your vicinity until you are pretty well able to handle them in a competent manner. Your instructor will work with you on those. If you have DME, and the VOR near you is a TACAN, you can include in your practice all the many VOR-DME approaches. And if (as at San Jose in the examples given here) your nearby VOR also has a full ILS system, you can add all ILS plates to your practice repertoire, except, of course, that you'll fly them as localizer approaches, without glide slope. Be sure to note that LOC minimums are different from ILS minimums with

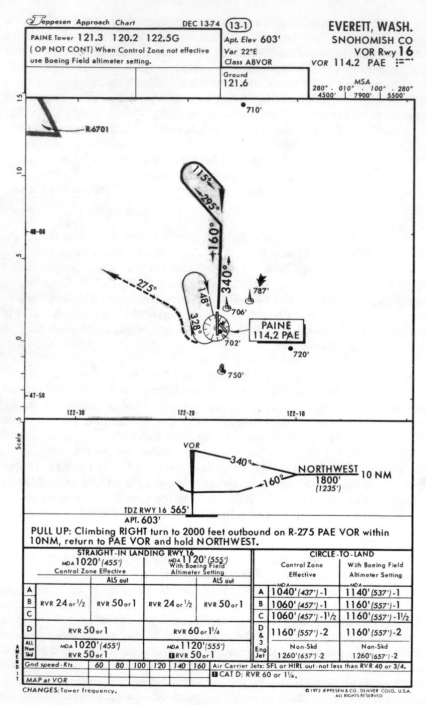

Fig. 7-5

glide slope—the approach plates give you this information. Finally, if you have ADF, and there is a nearby NDB, you can do simulated NDB approaches in just the same way (see Chapter 9).

Scoring for this exercise is exactly the same as for straight descents at approach airspeed, as in Chapter 6, with one addition: Any serious mis-interpretation of the approach plate gets an automatic 50 points—examples are flying a wrong radial, inbound or outbound; making a procedure turn on the wrong side of the approach course; or failing to initiate the descent to minimums at the appropriate point in the procedure.

Score Sheet: Simulated VOR Approaches.

ITEM	1	2	3	4	5	6	7	8	9	10
Session:										
Date:										
Total number of simulated approaches.										
Airspeed deviation greater than 5 knots. (10 points)										
——— greater than 10 knots. (20 additional)										
Altitude deviation in level flight or level-off greater than 50 ft. (10 points)										
——— greater than 100 ft. (20 additional)										
Vertical speed deviation greater than 50 ft/min. (10 points)										
——— greater than 100 ft/min. (20 additional)										
Failure to repeat clearance. (10 points)										
Misinterpretation of approach plate. (50 points)										
Descent below minimums. (50 points)										
Exceeding allowed elapsed time, or failure to start timing, or miscalculation of time. (50 points)										
Sloppy initiating of missed approach. (20 points)										
TOTAL POINT SCORE										
FINAL SCORE (= Total Point Score divided by total number of simulated approaches.)										

8. VOR HOLDING

Principles.

1. Definitions. (See Fig. 8-1)

Inbound leg = the magnetic course you fly **to** the holding fix.

Outbound leg = the magnetic course you fly **away from** the holding fix.

Nonholding side = the airspace on the side of the inbound leg that does not contain the outbound leg. For standard patterns (right turns) this will be the airspace to your left as you fly inbound.

Protected airspace = the airspace, at the specified altitude, which is sufficiently clear of terrain, and which ATC will keep clear of other IFR aircraft. The airspace beyond the fix end is not protected, and the airspace on the nonholding side is not protected. These facts determine entry procedures, any entry procedure being acceptable that does not let you blunder into unprotected airspace.

Direction to hold = the direction with relation to the fix, in which the holding pattern is to be located. This will always be the magnetic course of the outbound leg. In the diagram, the holding direction is southeast, and the clearance would read "Hold southeast of (fixname)."

2. Figuring out where to hold. You can hold at a navaid (VOR, ADF, compass locator) or at an enroute fix (intersection, DME fix).

At a navaid, you might be instructed to hold on any radial. Then the **inbound leg** is toward the navaid, on that radial. The **inbound course** will be the reciprocal of that radial.

At an enroute fix, you will usually be holding on an airway. At an intersection, you will always fly the inbound leg on the airway, toward the intersection. The reason is that you need accurate guidance on the inbound leg in order to arrive at the holding fix, and the airway provides that guidance. Fig. 8-2 gives some examples.

At a DME fix you could be instructed to hold on any radial, since the inbound leg would then be to or from the TACAN on a specified radial, providing the required accurate guidance, as shown in Fig. 8-3.

When you get a holding instruction, the first thing to do is to figure out the course for the **inbound leg** of the pattern, and draw it on your chart, as in Fig. 8-4.

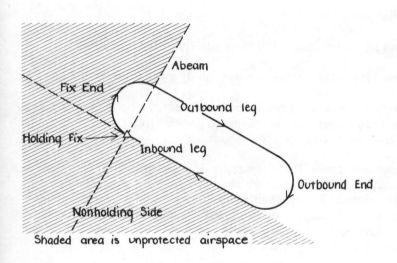

Fig. 8-1

Now you know your inbound leg. The next question is: When I complete the inbound leg, will I turn right or left at the fix? If there are no specific instructions, and nothing to the contrary is shown on the chart, make a standard pattern, right turns. Now draw in the rest of the pattern on the chart, as in Fig. 8-5.

Until you have absolute confidence in your proficiency, always draw the pattern on your chart, unless it is already shown there. It is amazingly easy to get confused and wander off into unprotected airspace—perhaps into a mountainside or another holding pattern.

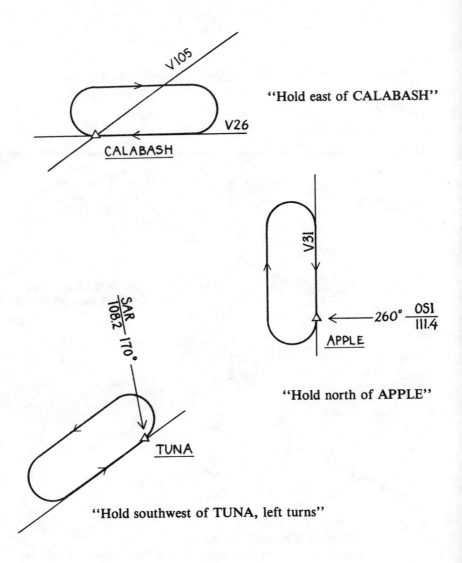

"Hold east of CALABASH"

"Hold north of APPLE"

"Hold southwest of TUNA, left turns"

Fig. 8-2

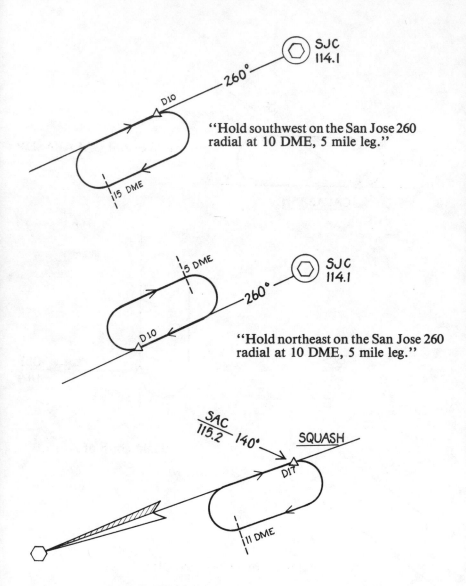

"Hold southwest on the San Jose 260 radial at 10 DME, 5 mile leg."

"Hold northeast on the San Jose 260 radial at 10 DME, 5 mile leg."

"Hold at SQUASH southwest."   or . . .
"Hold on the localizer, southwest of the 17 DME, 6 mile leg."

Fig. 8-3

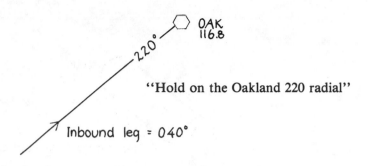

"Hold on the Oakland 220 radial"

Inbound leg = 040°

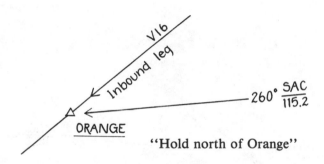

"Hold north of Orange"

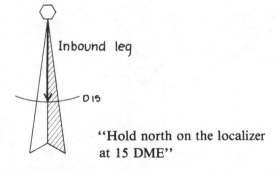

"Hold north on the localizer at 15 DME"

Fig. 8-4

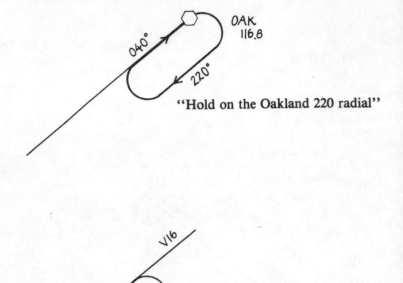

"Hold on the Oakland 220 radial"

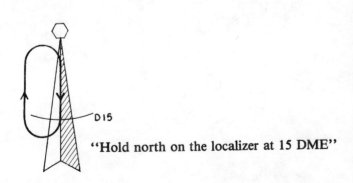

"Hold north of Orange, left turns"

"Hold north on the localizer at 15 DME"

Fig. 8-5

3. How to enter holding. Too much of a mystery has been made of this. The point is simply to enter the holding pattern in such a way that you remain in protected airspace. The simplest general procedure for this is to turn the shortest distance to the outbound course. Then you proceed by common sense, with reference to the pattern you have drawn (Fig. 8-6).

If the turn to the outbound course will put you pretty much **on** the outbound leg, you are all set. Just fly the pattern. This is called a **direct entry**.

If the turn to the outbound course will put you pretty much on the inbound leg, going the wrong way, fly outbound 1 minute, make a procedure turn on the holding side (the protected side), and intercept the inbound leg. Then fly the pattern. This is called a **parallel entry**.

If the turn to the outbound course will put you somewhere in the middle of the pattern, modify your entry as follows: Instead of turning to the outbound course, turn to a heading 30° less than the outbound course (30° more than, in a nonstandard left-turns pattern). Fly outbound 1 minute, then turn toward the inbound leg, intercept it, and fly the pattern. This is called a **teardrop entry**.

If you follow the principle of not violating unprotected airspace, the exact details of how to enter a holding pattern don't really matter much. The FAA recommendations are just that—recommendations—and for many pilots they may be more confusing than helpful. If you like to memorize numbers and procedures, you can follow the FAA rules, but be sure you understand what you're doing. In my opinion, if you know what you're doing, you're better off not cluttering your brain with rote procedures that have no immediately obvious logic to them. Anyway, here is how to do it the FAA way:

What is your present heading as you approach the fix?
What will be the **outbound course** in the pattern?

Add 70° to your heading. Does the resulting range, from your present heading to the heading plus 70° include the outbound course of the pattern? If so, make a **teardrop entry**.

Example: Your heading = 250°. Outbound course = 300°. 250 + 70 = 320. Range 250-320 includes 300.

If not, subtract 110° from your heading. Does that range now include the outbound course? If so, make a **parallel entry**.

Example: Your heading = 020°. Outbound course = 300°. 020 - 110 = 270. Range 020 counterclockwise to 270 includes 300.

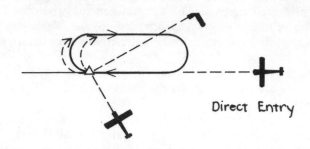

Direct Entry

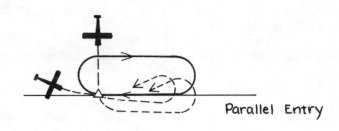

Parallel Entry

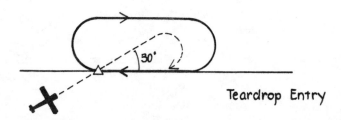

Teardrop Entry

Fig. 8-6

If neither of the above works, make a **direct entry**.

Example: Your heading = 110°. Outbound course = 300°. 110 + 70 = 180. 110 to 180 does not include 300.
110 - 110 = 360. 110 counterclockwise to 360 does not include 300.

For nonstandard (left turns) patterns, follow the same rule, but change "add" to "subtract", and "subtract" to "add".

If you have the type of DG that is vertically mounted and shows your heading at the top, there is an elegantly simple way of displaying pattern entries directly on it so that no computations are required. I am indebted to E. Schonburger of Norristown, Pa. for this idea. As shown in Fig. 8-7, make a permanent mark or affix a label 110 degrees around and to the left of the heading mark, and inscribe the word PARALLEL between it and the heading mark. Similarly, make a mark 70 degrees to the right of the heading mark, and inscribe the word TEARDROP in the corresponding position. Now as you approach the holding fix, locate the **outbound course** on your DG. If it is in the segment marked PARALLEL or that marked TEARDROP, that is the correct entry. If it is anywhere else, make a direct entry. This method has the real advantage that all the information is displayed visually on your primary reference instrument for heading.

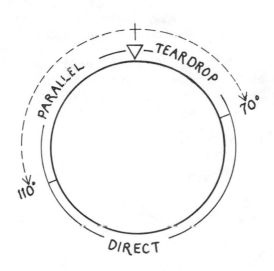

Fig. 8-7

4. How to fly the pattern. As soon as possible, set the OBS of one of your NAVs to the **inbound course**. Leave it that way, since every time you fly the inbound leg you will need accurate course guidance.

When you reach the fix: TIME, TURN, TALK, in that order. This means you first note the time (let's assume it is 12 past the hour) and write it down. Next turn to start your pattern entry; you will have worked out this turn in advance. Once you are well into your pattern entry and have everything under control, report to Center, giving the time you entered holding, and your altitude: "2345 Juliet entered holding at Orange, one two, five thousand." The time you first arrived at the fix, just before you turned to enter the pattern, was the time you entered holding.

Once in the pattern, reduce speed, and make clean standard rate turns. Start timing abeam the fix. If the fix is a VOR, the abeam position will be when the flag passes through OFF as it flips from TO to FROM. If the fix is a NDB, the needle will be at 90° or 270°. If the fix is an intersection, start timing as you roll out on the outbound heading. Time the outbound leg exactly 1 minute. Make your turn at the outbound end a clean standard rate turn until you see how the interception of the inbound course is working out. Remember, when you turn at the outbound end, you are always trying to intercept the inbound course. In no-wind conditions, if the turn at the fix end was exactly standard rate, a standard rate turn at the outbound end will put you exactly on the inbound course at rollout. So by the time you intercept the inbound course you should have a pretty good idea of the crosswind component, if any. If your standard rate turn at the outbound end works out just right, there is no crosswind. If you overshoot (Fig. 8-8, a) and have to continue the turn in order to intercept, the wind is from the holding side—it was drifting you toward the inbound leg during your outbound leg. If you undershoot (Fig. 8-8, b) and have to set up an intercept angle after your rollout because the needle didn't move in sufficiently, the wind is from the nonholding side—it was drifting you away from the inbound course during your outbound leg.

Start timing as soon as you complete the turn to the inbound heading, even if you haven't quite intercepted the inbound course. The whole point is to make finer and finer adjustments, each time around the pattern, so that the inbound leg will take just 1 minute. Try out a crab correction on the inbound leg, based on the result of your turn at the outbound end. Change the crab angle by small amounts, to keep the needle centered as you fly the inbound leg.

Crossing the fix inbound. VOR: Station passage = TO-FROM reversal. NDB: Station passage = ADF needle reversal. Intersection: Have your second NAV set for the intersection, so the needle will center at the intersection. DME: Self-evident. In all cases note the time at fix passage and start turn to outbound.

You should now have a pretty good idea of the headwind/tailwind component and the crosswind component.

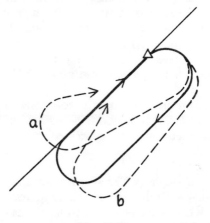

Fig. 8-8

Correcting for headwind/tailwind: Time the outbound leg longer or shorter than 1 minute by an amount equal to the error on the inbound leg. For example, if your inbound leg took 1 min 20 sec, you had a headwind, so you will have a tailwind outbound. Shorten the outbound by 20 sec, i.e., fly outbound only 40 sec. Suppose, on the other hand, your inbound leg took only 35 sec, or 25 sec less than you wanted. In that case add 25 sec to your outbound leg and fly outbound 1 min 25 sec. On each circuit this process can be refined, until your inbound leg works out exactly at 1 minute.

Correcting for crosswind: Here you have determined by trial what crab angle is necessary to keep you on the inbound course. Your crab for the outbound leg will have to be 2 to 3 times greater, since the same crosswind acts on you throughout both 1-minute turns, as well as during the outbound leg itself, whereas it acts for only 1 minute inbound. A simple rule is to double the crab for the outbound leg, and refine this on each circuit. You will know you are right when the standard rate turn at the outbound end rolls you right onto the inbound course. Remember where the crosswind is coming from; if you had to crab left flying inbound, you'll have to crab right flying outbound.

In a few circuits of the pattern you should have everything working smoothly, with finer and finer corrections. Of course, if the wind changes, you'll have to modify your corrections.

5. How to leave the pattern. Be sure you get an expect further clearance (EFC) or expect approach clearance (EAC) time **before** you enter holding. Without this you'd be in real trouble if you had a communication failure while holding.

When you are cleared to leave the pattern in order to proceed on your route, arrange to leave the holding fix as nearly as possible to the specified time. You do this simply by shortening the outbound, or lengthening it, as required. Since the whole pattern takes approximately 4 minutes, you can judge this maneuver quite easily. Departing the holding fix is a compulsory report to ATC: "45 Juliet departed holding at 43."

Communications failure. In this situation you simply arrange to leave holding at the EFC (or EAC) time and proceed according to your last clearance or the flight planned route, as prescribed in the general rules for communications failure.

6. Holding with a single NAV. If your airplane only has one NAV you'll become familiar with this exercise early in your IFR training. If you have two NAV receivers, you can expect to have this thrown at you during your IFR check ride. The principles are simple and logical, but they require some practice.

Holding at a VOR only requires one NAV anyway, so the exercise is only meaningful for intersection holding. And there's no problem on the outbound leg, since you fly that by heading and time. What the problem boils down to, then, is to fly inbound with the needle centered and the NAV tuned to the VOR you use for primary course guidance, and at the same time to know accurately when you arrive at the intersection. The procedure is therefore exactly the same as that for flying along an airway with a single NAV, and identifying your arrival at an intersection. Once established on the inbound course (i.e., toward the intersection) with needle centered, note your heading on the DG. Hold that heading, and switch to the VOR frequency and OBS setting corresponding to the intersection. If the needle is pointing toward the station, you haven't arrived at the intersection yet. If the needle is considerably off center, switch back again to your course-guidance VOR and fly a while longer, correcting any deviation by a slight heading change. Then switch again to the intersection VOR. Once the needle is moving in toward the center, hold your heading until it centers. Now you are at the intersection. Turn to the outbound heading, return to your course-guidance VOR, and set the OBS for the inbound course again. Remember to identify each VOR station **every time you switch,** to avoid any possibility of switching to a wrong frequency.

Practice.

Your check pilot has to be inventive, to present you with all sorts of holding patterns requiring different entry procedures. Climb to 3000 feet above a VOR, as in the previous chapter. Start with holding on various radials at the VOR.

Check pilot: "2345 Juliet hold at San Jose on the 330 radial. Expect further clearance at 55. Maintain 3000."

You: Acknowledge and proceed. Tune in the VOR, center the needle with the indicator showing TO, turn to the inbound heading, identify the VOR during your turn, center the needle once after you've completed your turn, then fly direct to the VOR, using the tracking procedures you now know so well. As you proceed inbound, sketch the holding pattern. Holding on the 330 radial means your **inbound** course will be on that radial, i.e., your inbound course will be 330 - 180 = 150 degrees. Your outbound course will be 330 degrees, after you make a right turn at the VOR. From your outbound course and your present heading compute the type of pattern entry you'll need. Crossing the VOR, note the time, make your entry, and report to Center: "2345 Juliet entered holding at San Jose, 44, level at 3000."

Reduce power to a comfortable endurance range, retrim for level flight at the new power setting, then fly at least three circuits of the pattern, sharpening it up on each circuit. The final circuit should be perfect, with the crab correction hammered down, and the inbound leg taking exactly one minute. When your check pilot gives you a new clearance to proceed, e.g., "2345 cleared to depart San Jose on the 330 radial, flight planned route," be prepared to shorten the pattern as required to leave the VOR as soon as possible, or at the specified time, if that has been stated.

Then your check pilot should let you fly outbound for a few minutes, then give you a new holding pattern at the same VOR: "2345 Juliet cleared direct San Jose, hold on the 060 radial, left turns, maintain 3000."

When you have mastered holding at a VOR, your check pilot should give you clearances to hold at a nearby intersection on an airway. Both the airway and the intersection can be invented and given to you, for example: "Victor 35 is the 190 radial from San Jose. RADISH intersection is defined by the Woodside 100 radial (or the 10 DME fix, or whatever). Hold north at RADISH." Intersection holding presents no remarkable problems. After you do a few successfully, your check pilot should unexpectedly turn off one of your NAVs. This presents a considerable challenge until you get used to it.

Finally, and most difficult, are intersections defined by ADF, because then you have to compute the relative bearing at the intersection, taking into account your crab angle. ADF procedures are presented in detail in the next chapter.

Scoring is based primarily on your correctly working out and carrying out pattern entries. The most common problems lead to the most dangerous situations, such as confusing the inbound and outbound course and blundering off into unprotected airspace, or getting so disoriented that you fly out of the pattern altogether. Once in the pattern, you may be penalized for lack of smoothness, but you're not likely to do anything really dangerous. Altitude control will be a problem until you become very comfortable with the whole holding procedure, so you'll be penalized for altitude deviations as in previous exercises. The Score Sheet summarizes what you can expect.

Score Sheet

ITEM	1	2	3	4	5	6	7	8	9	10
Session:										
Date:										
Total number of holding patterns flown (3 circuits each, on the average).										
Incorrect entry procedure. (20 points)										
Serious violation of unprotected airspace. (50 points)										
Failure to report entering holding. (10 points)										
Failure to time. (20 points)										
Poor interception turning inbound. (10 points)										
Poor crab corrections. (10 points)										
Poor headwind/tailwind corrections. (10 points)										
Failure to reduce speed in pattern. (10 points)										
Altitude deviation greater than 50 ft. (10 points)										
—— greater than 100 ft. (20 additional)										
Blundering procedure with single NAV. (20 points)										
Failure to report leaving holding. (10 points)										
Failure to repeat a clearance or to obtain an EFC or EAC time. (10 points)										
TOTAL POINT SCORE										
FINAL SCORE (= Total Point Score divided by total number of holding patterns flown.)										

9. ADF PROCEDURES

Inbound and Outbound Tracking.

Principles. ADF receivers can tune radiobeacons in the low-frequency band (approximately 200-500 KHz) as well as broadcast stations in the 500-1500 KHz band. IFR procedures using ADF are based on low-frequency radiobeacons, the frequencies and identifiers of which are shown on the appropriate navigational charts. Ordinarily—and for actual IFR flying—you will be using these low-frequency radiobeacons. For practice, however, as well as for backup in crosscountry flying, AM broadcast transmitters make excellent NDB's. Many of these are shown on the sectional charts together with their frequencies and call signs. If you have digital tuning on your ADF, you can use such a station quite easily without much chance of error, since an identical frequency is not assigned to more than one station in a given geographic area. Without digital tuning—and for absolute certainty anyway—you'll have to wait for station identification, and this may take as long as 15 minutes. A very useful adjunct to ADF flying is **White's Radio Log**, which lists all AM broadcast stations by location and frequency. This can be obtained from the publishers of Communications World (Davis Publications, Inc., 229 Park Avenue South, New York, N. Y. 10003).

There are five kinds of procedure involving ADF: (1) Intercepting a magnetic bearing **to** the nondirectional radiobeacon (NDB) and tracking it inbound. This is analogous to intercepting and tracking a VOR radial inbound to the omni station. (2) Intercepting a magnetic bearing **from** the NDB and tracking it outbound. This is analogous to intercepting and tracking a radial outbound from a VOR. Magnetic bearings **from** a NDB are exactly analogous to radials from a VOR. (3) Flying a holding pattern based on a NDB. (4) Recognizing an intersection that is specified by a magnetic bearing to a NDB, or establishing your position by finding the magnetic bearing from yourself to a NDB. (5) ADF approaches.

The basic principle of ADF is very simple. The ADF needle always points directly to the NDB. In this respect it is very different from the needle of your VOR-NAV display, which tells you what radial you are on, but is indifferent to your heading. If you are on the 165 radial from a VOR, and your OBS is set to 165, the indicator will show FROM, and the needle will be centered. If you now execute a 360 degree turn, the needle will remain centered throughout, assuming you are far enough from the station so that you don't get onto the 164 or 166 radial during the turn. If you do the same maneuver with ADF, the result is entirely different. First, let's assume you are on the 165 radial from the ADF (i.e., a line of magnetic bearing 165 degrees from the NDB will touch your airplane), and your heading is 165. Then the ADF needle will point directly at your tail, toward the NDB; it will actually point downward at 180 degrees on the panel display, since 360 degrees represents the nose of the ship, 180 degrees the tail, 90 degrees the line extending out the right wing, and 270 degrees the line extending out the left wing. Now if you execute a 360 degree turn to the right, the ADF needle will continue pointing at the NDB throughout your turn. Thus, as you begin the turn to the right, it will show 170, then 160, and so on, until when you are facing the station it will point upright to 360, then continue swinging through 350, 340, and eventually back to 180 as you roll out of your turn. This is shown in Fig. 9-1. To fly ADF smoothly, you have to understand which way the needle will go as you turn one way or the other, and therefore, which way to turn in order to correct for wind drift.

Flying a short distance to a NDB is a trivial exercise called **homing**. You put the needle on the nose (straight up, 360 degrees on the scale) and keep it there until you cross the NDB, indicated by the needle swinging from nose to tail as you leave the beacon behind. You don't bother making crab corrections for wind drift, since the distance is short; you may have to change heading to keep the needle on the nose, so your flight path may be slightly curved instead of straight, but you'll get there in a few minutes all the same. This situation would arise, typically, in a transition from an airway to a NDB preparatory to an approach. An example is shown in Fig. 9-2—the ILS Rwy 29R approach at Stockton, California, where the outer marker on the localizer course is a compass locator (NDB). An airway crosses the Stockton (SCK) VOR 1.7 miles away. You would normally make the transition by flying the airway to the VOR, then flying the ADF needle directly to the outer compass locator and entering the specified holding pattern prior to the final phase of the approach.

Usually, however, the aim is to track a straight line to a NDB, perhaps over a considerable distance. Then correcting for wind drift becomes essential. First tune the NDB with the ADF selector switch in ANTenna position (on some instruments marked SELector), identify it aurally by its code identifier, then switch to ADF position to activate the needle. Turn the ship the shortest distance toward the needle, and roll out with the needle on the nose (straight up, 360 degrees on the scale). Now note your heading on the DG. As always in tracking procedures, you fly a definite heading, using the ADF needle to monitor whether or not it is correct, just as you would do tracking inbound to a VOR. Let's suppose your heading is 080 when you roll out with the needle on the nose. After flying for a while, holding this

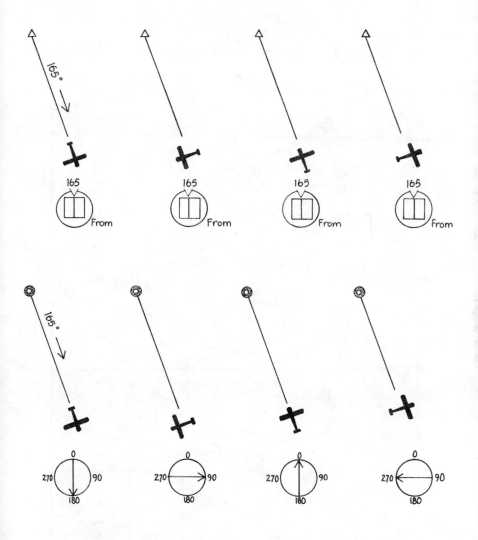

Fig. 9-1

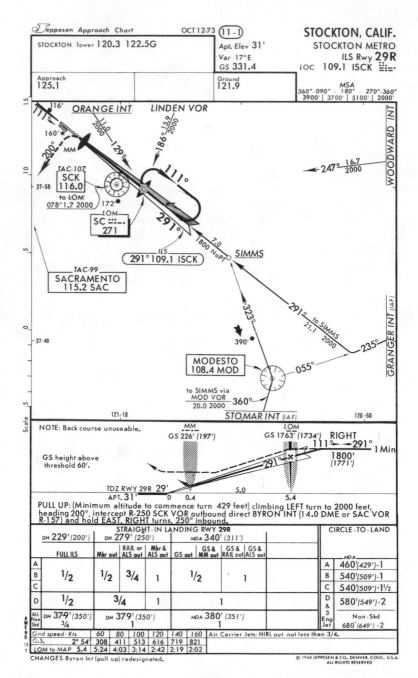

Fig. 9-2

heading exactly, you notice that the ADF needle has drifted to the right, so it is now pointing 10 degrees to the right of the nose. Obviously the wind has drifted you to the left (unless your DG has precessed!), and you have a right crosswind component. So you have to crab to the right, toward the needle. But how much? You solve this problem by a simple trial-and-error maneuver. Double the deviation of the ADF needle. Since it is 10 degrees off, turn right 20 degrees. When you have done this, the needle will be pointing 10 degrees to the **left** of the nose. Now watch what happens. If your crab is too great, the needle will move farther to the left. If this happens, take out half of the crab correction—in this case change your heading 10 degrees to the left. If the needle starts moving to the right again, increase your crab angle to the right. The aim of all this is to stop the needle. When this has finally been accomplished, you will be tracking inbound in a straight line, your crab correction will be just right to compensate for wind drift, and the needle will be pointing to the left of the nose by **exactly the same number of degrees as your crab angle** to the right. This is shown in Fig. 9-3.

Another way of describing this situation is to say that the sum of your heading plus the relative bearing on the ADF needle is equal to the course you are tracking. In other words, add your two instrument readings (the DG and the ADF needle) to get your magnetic bearing. In Fig. 9-3, at left, your heading (090) plus the relative bearing (minus 10 degrees) equals 080, the inbound bearing. In the same illustration, at right, your heading (065) plus relative bearing (015) equals 080, the same inbound bearing. Note that relative bearings to the right of the nose position are considered positive, those to the left are measured as negative. This is simpler than adding and then subtracting 360 degrees, e.g., 090 + 350 = 440; 440 − 360 = 080.

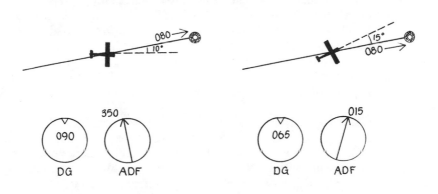

Fig. 9-3

As in tracking a VOR radial inbound, so here too, the art of making a smooth station passage is to recognize that the closer you get to the station, the smaller your corrections have to be, and the sooner you have to observe and detect small needle deviations. The only difference—and it's a minor one—is that in VOR tracking the needle is always kept stationary in the center position, whereas in ADF tracking the needle is kept stationary in the position corresponding to the crab angle.

Intercepting a magnetic bearing to a NDB is very simple. Suppose you want to intercept the 260 bearing **to** the station (in VOR terminology this would be intercepting the 080 radial and flying it inbound). First, turn the ship to 260. Now you are obviously parallel to the bearing you want to fly on. The only question is: "Where is it?" The ADF needle tells you. If it points left, the bearing you want is to the left; if it points right, that bearing is to the right. If it points straight ahead, you are on it. Suppose the needle points 20 degrees to the left of the nose. As in making crab corrections, double the deviation, in this case turning 40 degrees to the left. Now the needle will point 20 degrees to the **right**. You are making a 40 degree intercept of the bearing you want. How will you know when you get there? As Fig. 9-4 shows, when you reach that bearing, the NDB will be 40 degrees to your right.

So the rule is: When the ADF needle shows the same angle off your nose as the intercept angle you set up, you are there. Turn toward the station, roll out with the needle on your nose and the inbound heading on your DG, and continue the inbound tracking exercise as before. In these interception maneuvers, never get so absorbed doubling numbers that you exceed the maximum permissible intercept angle, which is obviously 90 degrees, since beyond that you'd be flying backwards from where you want to go.

When you intercept an inbound course, you automatically get a time-to-the-station estimate. Study the diagram, and you'll see that the intercept leg and the inbound leg from the point of interception will always be equal—they are two sides of an isosceles triangle. This means that if you start timing from your turn to the intercept angle, and stop timing when you intercept the inbound course, your time will be exactly the same as the time remaining until you reach the NDB, ignoring wind effects.

Time-to-station estimates, in general, are very easy with ADF. The steps are basically the same as with VOR, so you should review the description in Chapter 7. First, turn toward the NDB, so the needle is on your nose. Second, turn 80 degrees right or left. Start timing, maintain the heading exactly, and time until the needle has moved 10 degrees toward your tail. Immediately turn inbound toward the station. Divide the elapsed time in seconds by 10 to get the estimated time to the station in minutes. Add this to the actual time, to get an ETA at the radiobeacon. Fly to the station and see how good your estimate was.

Intercepting magnetic bearings and flying them outbound is really no different, provided you keep in mind which way you're travelling. The interception procedure is exactly the same. Set up the heading you want, parallel to the outbound bearing you want to track. Then set up an intercept angle that is double the needle deviation. Now, however, the needle is pointing in the general direction of your tail, and as you set up your intercept angle, it will deviate **even more** in the same direction. But the basic principle still holds: When the needle eventually points away from the tail at an angle equal to your intercept angle, you have just intercepted the magnetic bearing you want. Turn outbound to place the needle directly on your tail (straight down, 180 degrees), and start the regular outbound tracking procedure described below.

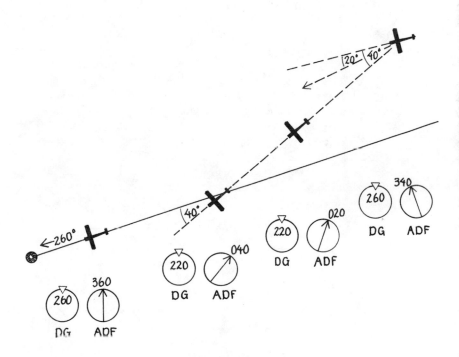

Fig. 9-4

Outbound tracking works the same as inbound tracking, except that when you make crab corrections the needle deviation will become greater rather than smaller. Suppose you are flying outbound on a bearing of 150 from the NDB, and you start out with the needle pointing directly at your tail, as in Fig. 9-5. After a while the needle points 5 degrees to the right of the tail (i.e., 175 degrees on the ADF indicator). Obviously, the wind has drifted you to the left, and you have to crab to the right. Doubling the deviation means crabbing 10 degrees to the right. But now the needle will point 15 degrees to the right. From here on, the procedure is just the same as when tracking inbound. The aim is first to get back on course. This will be accomplished when the needle deviation is equal to your crab angle, which is really an intercept angle. This is the same criterion for knowing you had intercepted your desired bearing in the earlier interception exercises.

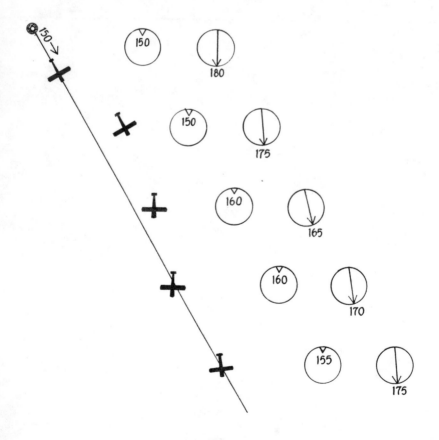

Fig. 9-5

In this case, you will be on course when the needle is 10 degrees to the right of the tail. Now if you maintain the same heading, you'll cross the course, since the needle is still moving. The second step, therefore, after getting on course, is to stop the needle. That means taking out some of the crab angle. A good place to begin is to take out half of what you started with. Here, you'd take out 5 degrees. This will put you on a heading of 155, and the needle will be pointing 5 degrees to the right of the tail (175 degrees on its own scale, or minus 5 degrees with respect to the tail index). If the needle moves no more, you know everything is correct. You want to be on the 150 bearing outbound, your heading is 155, and the needle deviation is the same as your crab angle. Adding, as before: $155 + (-5) = 150$. If the needle drifts again, repeat the maneuver, using smaller corrections each time.

We can summarize the principles of ADF tracking, whether inbound or outbound, as follows:

(1) To intercept a desired magnetic bearing:
    (a) Turn to parallel the bearing.
    (b) Note the needle deviation.
    (c) Set up an intercept angle twice the needle deviation but no greater than 90 degrees.
    (d) Fly the intercept heading until the needle deviation equals the intercept angle.
    (e) Turn inbound or outbound as desired, placing the needle on the nose or on the tail.

(2) To track inbound or outbound on a magnetic bearing:
    (a) Fly the correct heading, with the needle on nose or tail.
    (b) Observe the needle closely to detect the first definite deviation.
    (c) Turn toward the needle, setting up a crab angle double the needle deviation.
    (d) If the needle deviates more, increase the crab angle.
    (e) When the needle movement reverses, you are returning to your course; continue the same heading until the needle deviation equals your crab angle, then you are again on course.
    (f) Take out half of the crab correction.
    (g) Continue by trial-and-error, making small crab changes, so as to keep the needle stationary with the needle deviation equal to the crab correction, the condition associated with being on the chosen magnetic bearing with the correct wind drift correction.

Practice. Find a NDB where you can practice at a safe altitude. If it is a compass locator on an ILS approach course, be sure you practice well above the altitude at which the approach path crosses the NDB. Usually, when the NDB is collocated with the outer marker, this will be approximately 1500 feet above the airport elevation. So 3000 feet above the airport should be a safe altitude. Alternatively, a nearby AM broadcast station can be chosen for use as a NDB, as previously described. In either case, tune and identify the station before using it.

Begin by tracking directly to the NDB by the simple "homing" method of keeping the needle on the nose. You can assess how cleanly you make station passage by how sharply the needle swings from nose to tail when you cross the beacon. The farther off to one side you are, the more slowly will the reversal take place. When you have crossed the NDB, fly outbound along a definite line of magnetic bearing ("radial"). Your check pilot should give you the instruction, starting by choosing radials that are close to the heading you are already flying.

> Check Pilot: "2345 Juliet track outbound the 175 radial from HAYWARD. (Note that all NDB's have names.) Maintain 3000."
> You: "45 Juliet track outbound the 175 radial from HAYWARD. Maintain 3000."

Turn to 175 to parallel the desired radial, set up your intercept angle, and continue as described earlier.

> C.P.: "2345 Juliet report intercepting the 175 radial from HAYWARD."
> You: "45 Juliet report intercepting the 175 radial from HAYWARD."

And when you've intercepted and turned outbound, heading 175, and the ADF needle is on the tail—

> You: "45 Juliet established on the HAYWARD 175 outbound, level at 3."
> C.P.: "Roger, 45 Juliet."

Now fly outbound for long enough to allow time for wind drift to take effect and for you to set up appropriate crab corrections. Once your check pilot knows where the wind is coming from, he should set you up as much as possible in crosswind conditions to give you maximum practice in making corrections.

After you've flown outbound about 5 minutes, your check pilot should have you turn and intercept a magnetic bearing inbound. Usually it should be within 30 or 40 degrees of where you are.

> C.P.: "2345 Juliet intercept and track inbound the 320 bearing to HAYWARD, report established on course, maintain 3000."

You acknowledge and proceed to do it. You're flying outbound 175, that's roughly 180, and you have to turn to 320 first, that's a turn to the right. Roll out on 320. The ADF needle is pointing to the right. Set up an intercept angle to the right, and continue as described earlier.

You can get a lot of practice in a short time by continuing the sequence: track inbound, cross the station, intercept an outbound radial, track outbound, turn and intercept a bearing inbound, and so on. When you become very comfortable with this, and pretty skillful, your check pilot can add some climbs and descents. At first, these are given during the phases of the exercise when you are established on course and have little to do but monitor the needle and make small corrections in crab angle. Later, more challenge can be introduced by calling out the climbs and descents to coincide with interceptions or station passage. Occasionally, a time-to-station estimate should be called for.

Scoring follows familiar lines. You'll be penalized for making S-turns across your desired magnetic bearing rather than holding a steady course, unintended heading changes greater than 10 degrees, sloppy station passage, wrong procedures or total confusion (this may happen in the beginning), altitude deviations, and failure to repeat clearances or to make required reports. Sessions should not exceed 30 minutes. See Score Sheet, page 9-12.

ADF Holding at NDB.

Principles. A holding pattern in which the holding fix is a NDB presents no special problems once the ADF tracking procedures described in the previous section have been mastered. The magnetic bearing inbound to the NDB is always given in the procedure. So you track inbound on the specified bearing, cross the station, make a standard rate turn to the right, roll out on the appropriate heading (reciprocal of the inbound bearing), start timing when the NDB is abeam (needle pointing at the right wing), fly one minute outbound, turn right again and intercept the inbound bearing. The first time you do this inbound interception, you'll find out about any crosswind component. If you roll out onto the inbound heading and the needle is pointing at the nose, you have no crosswind. Otherwise, you'll have the usual crab corrections to set up, just as described for tracking procedures. Then on the outbound leg you'll put in double the correction,

Score Sheet: Inbound and Outbound Tracking.

ITEM	1	2	3	4	5	6	7	8	9	10
Session:										
Date:										
Total number of outbound trackings plus total number of inbound trackings.										
Failure to intercept correctly, or other wrong procedures. (10 points)										
Failure to hold steady course on desired bearing, or S-turns across bearing. (10 points)										
Unintended heading changes greater than 10°. (10 points)										
Sloppy station passage. (10 points)										
Total confusion. (10 points)										
Incorrect procedure in time-to-station estimate. (10 points)										
Altitude deviation greater than 50 ft. (10 points)										
—— greater than 100 ft. (20 additional)										
Failure to repeat clearances. (10 points)										
Failure to make required reports. (10 points)										
TOTAL POINT SCORE										
FINAL SCORE (= Total Point Score divided by sum of outbound and inbound trackings.)										

following all the same principles you've learned already for holding at a VOR or an intersection.

Practice. Your check pilot should give you various holding patterns, both standard and left-turns, and on various magnetic bearings to the NDB. Pattern entries follow exactly the same principles you've learned already.

> C.P.: "2345 Juliet hold at HAYWARD, 210 degrees inbound, expect further clearance at 16, maintain 3000."

You acknowledge, then proceed to your first step, which is to fly directly to the NDB. When you're established on an inbound heading, draw a picture to help you visualize how you'll be approaching the NDB, and how you'll make the pattern entry. From then on, it's the same procedure you've practiced to perfection with VOR holding patterns.

Scoring follows exactly the same principles as with VOR holding patterns. Smoothness is the aim, with complete control of the aircraft while tracing the pattern accurately and compensating for crosswind and headwind/tailwind components. See Score Sheet, page 9-14.

ADF Intersections and Intersection Holding.

Principles. An ADF intersection is defined by the magnetic bearing **to** the NDB. The custom is thus exactly the opposite of that for a VOR intersection, which is always defined by the VOR radial, i.e., the magnetic bearing **from** the VOR. As you have learned already, the sum of the readings on your two panel instruments (the DG and the ADF needle) gives you the bearing to the NDB. Stated as an equation: heading + relative bearing = magnetic bearing to the station.

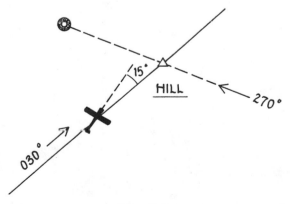

Fig. 9-6

Score Sheet: ADF Holding at NDB.

ITEM	1	2	3	4	5	6	7	8	9	10
Session:										
Date:										
Total number of holding patterns flown (3 circuits each, on the average.)										
Incorrect entry procedure. (20 points)										
Serious violation of unprotected airspace. (50 points)										
Failure to report entering holding. (20 points)										
Failure to time. (20 points)										
Poor interception turning inbound. (10 points)										
Poor crab corrections. (10 points)										
Poor headwind/tailwind corrections. (10 points)										
Failure to reduce speed in pattern. (10 points)										
Altitude deviation greater than 50 ft. (10 points)										
—— greater than 100 ft. (20 additional)										
Failure to report leaving holding. (10 points)										
Failure to repeat a clearance or to obtain an EFC or EAC time. (10 points)										
TOTAL POINT SCORE										
FINAL SCORE (= Total Point Score divided by total number of holding patterns flown.)										

Consider the example in Fig. 9-6. The airway course is 030, and HILL intersection is defined, as shown, by a bearing of 270 to the NDB. Without a crosswind, your heading would be 030, so you would be at HILL when 030 plus your relative bearing (shown by the ADF needle) equaled 270, i.e., when your ADF needle showed 240. Suppose, however, that you are carrying a crab angle, say 15 degrees to the left, as shown, so your DG shows 015 instead of 030. Then 015 + rel. bearing = 270, and your ADF will show 255 at HILL.

Often it is easiest to consider how many degrees the ADF needle will point to the left or right of the nose or tail index, rather than doing the arithmetic outlined above. In Fig. 9-7, if your heading is 280 and the bearing to the NDB at VALLEY intersection will be 260, it is obvious that the needle must point 20 degrees to the left of the nose, in other words, to 340. This is so clear at a glance, that it seems foolish to become involved in

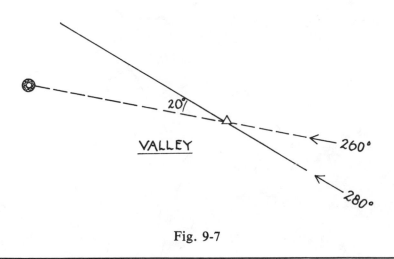

Fig. 9-7

solving the equation 380 + rel. bearing = 260. If you do solve the equation, remember you have to add 360 whenever necessary to let you subtract a larger number from a smaller one. Thus, rel. bearing = 260 — 280 = 360 + 260 — 280 = 340.

The safest way to do all these ADF intersection problems is to draw a diagram, right on the IFR chart if necessary, writing in the relative bearing for the no-wind condition. Then you have only to add or subtract your crab angle, referring to the diagram for this step too. What is most important is to use your diagram to **understand** the procedure; then if calculation gives you an absurd answer, you'll recognize it before acting on it.

The method of thinking the procedure through—some people even do it out loud, talking themselves through it—is seen in the following example. As shown in Fig. 9-8, you are tracking V27 on a course of 345, and your DG shows a heading of 352. PINE intersection is defined by a magnetic bearing of 030 to the NDB. How will you know when you are at PINE? Here is what you might go through: I am on the airway, and if there were no wind, my heading would be 345. At PINE, 345 + rel. bearing = 030, so the ADF needle would show 45° to the right of the nose index, i.e., 045 on the ADF scale. But I am crabbing 7° to the right. That means the needle will deviate 7° less from the nose index, i.e., it will show 38° relative bearing.

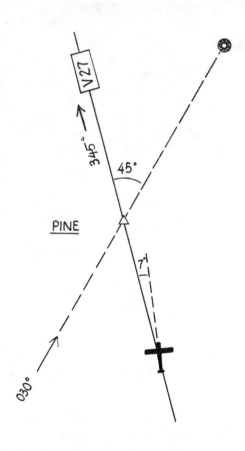

Fig. 9-8

A modern type of ADF indicator is provided with an outer 360-degree scale, which can be rotated by a knob, to correspond to your DG indication. Then the ADF needle will give the magnetic bearing to the NDB directly, since all the arithmetic will be done mechanically. An example is shown in Fig. 9-9. The heading has been set manually to 060, the NDB is 45 degrees to the right of the nose, and the bearing to the NDB is 105°. The disadvantage of the rotating outer scale is that you have to change it by hand every time you change your heading. Thus, there is some danger you may forget to do this, but use the instrument anyway, in an unthinking and automatic way.

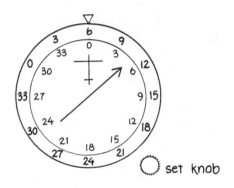

Fig. 9-9

Obtaining a line of bearing to a NDB for the purpose of locating your position on the sectional chart in VFR flying follows exactly the same principle. Note your heading and the deviation of the ADF needle, and it is a simple matter to compute the bearing to the NDB. Suppose, as in Fig. 9-10, your heading is 190 and the ADF needle is pointing to 155 on its own scale. The station is behind you and to your right. A quick sketch gives the correct magnetic bearing to the station. Here 190 (your heading) **plus** 155 (the relative bearing on the ADF) gives 345, the magnetic bearing to the NDB.

Practice. The best and cheapest practice for ADF intersections can be obtained on the ground. No attempt should be made to practice in the air until all the confusion has subsided and you are able to make the calculations quickly, calmly, and accurately. Then, and only then, should your check pilot put you through a series of exercises, both on ADF intersections (reporting them) and holding patterns based on an ADF intersection as holding fix.

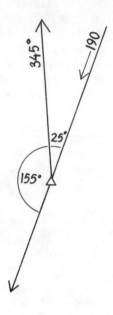

Fig. 9-10

You'll need both a VOR and a NDB for this exercise. Fly an actual airway based on the VOR, or invent one, so that you're tracking away from or toward (away from is easier!) the VOR. Ideally, you should be more than 10 miles from the VOR at first; as you become more skillful, you can try it closer in, where you'll have to work harder to stay on your airway, while also figuring out where the intersection is. When you're established on the real or simulated airway, your check pilot has to start inventing intersections. He should simply include their description in each simulated command. Let's suppose you're tracking outbound on the 100 radial from a VOR, maintaining 3000 feet, and that HAYWARD radiobeacon is over to your left. In order to avoid giving you nonsensical instructions, your check pilot should work out the angles on a sheet of paper, at least approximately, before calling them out.

> C.P.: "2345 Juliet report ABEL intersection, bearing 080 to HAYWARD."

After you acknowledge this, you sketch the situation on paper. Your heading is 100 (assuming no wind), at ABEL the bearing to HAYWARD will be 080, that's just 20 degrees to your left. Right now the needle is probably only a few degrees to the left, but as you continue on course, it will move down more to the left. When it has moved 20 degrees (showing 340 on its own scale), you report.

> You: "45 Juliet at ABEL, level at 3."
> C.P.: "45 Juliet, Roger. Report BAKER intersection, bearing 010 HAYWARD."

And you make the calculation. Perhaps now you are crabbing 5 degrees to the left, so that your heading is 095. At BAKER, the bearing to the NDB will be 010, or 085 to the left of your nose. When you get there, report.

But your check pilot can throw a curve at you before you get to BAKER.

> C.P.: "2345 Juliet hold at BAKER, west, left turns, expect further clearance at 55."

Since you're to hold west, it will be a direct entry, for you're already heading east, and "hold west" means "hold on the west side of the fix". So you can't cross the fix. All you have to do when you reach the intersection is turn left, and you'll be in the pattern. Then each time you come around, you'll identify the intersection the same way—the angular distance from your heading to 010 (the bearing to the NDB) will be the deviation of the needle from your nose. As you reach BAKER and start your left turn, note the time, and remember to report:

> You: "45 Juliet entered holding at BAKER, 43 (the time), 3000."
> C.P.: "Roger 45 Juliet. Depart BAKER at 47."

Scoring follows the usual system. You'll be penalized for miscalculating the intersection, for failing to recognize it when you get there, for failing to report it, for errors in entering and flying the holding pattern, for poor altitude control, and for confused and sloppy technique. Separate score sheets are provided for ADF intersection work and for holding patterns based on ADF intersections. See pages 9-20 and 9-21.

Simulated ADF Approaches.

Principles. An ADF approach uses a NDB as part of the approach procedure, so that ADF equipment is essential to executing the approach. The NDB may be on the field; then the approach is exactly like a VOR approach with the VOR on the field, the final approach course being a magnetic course to the radiobeacon. The NDB may be off the airport—

Score Sheet: ADF Intersections.

Session:	1	2	3	4	5	6	7	8	9	10		
Date:												
ITEM												
Total number of intersections assigned.												
Incorrect computation of relative bearing. (20 points)												
Failure to fly precise heading at moment intersection identified. (20 points)												
Incorrect recognition of arrival at intersection. (20 points)												
Failure to report intersection. (10 points)												
Failure to repeat clearance. (10 points)												
Altitude deviation greater than 50 ft. (10 points)												
––– greater than 100 ft. (20 additional)												
TOTAL POINT SCORE												
FINAL SCORE (= Total Point Score divided by total number of intersections assigned.)												

Score Sheet: Holding at an ADF Intersection.

ITEM	1	2	3	4	5	6	7	8	9	10
Session:										
Date:										
Total number of holding patterns flown (3 circuits each, on the average.)										
Incorrect entry procedure. (20 points)										
Serious violation of unprotected airspace. (50 points)										
Failure to report entering holding. (10 points)										
Failure to time. (20 points)										
Poor interception turning inbound. (10 points)										
Poor crab correct ons. (10 points)										
Poor headwind/tailwind corrections. (10 points)										
Failure to reduce speed in pattern. (10 points)										
Altitude deviation greater than 50 ft. (10 points)										
— — greater than 100 ft. (20 additional)										
Failure to report leaving holding. (10 points)										
Failure to repeat a clearance or obtain an EFC or EAC time. (10 points)										
TOTAL POINT SCORE										
FINAL SCORE (= Total Point Score divided by total number of holding patterns flown.)										

often it is the outer marker (compass locator) on an ILS—and then the final approach course is a magnetic course from the radiobeacon, with timing to the missed approach point. In both these cases the approach simply applies the principles of tracking inbound or outbound, combined with the descent as specified in the profile view on the approach plate. ADF intersections may also play a role on an ADF approach. For example, an ADF intersection may be part of the transition from the airway to the approach course, or it might even provide a back-up indication of a missed approach point. Other than these specific ways that a NDB may be used instead of a VOR, the principles of flying ADF approaches are exactly the same as for flying VOR approaches.

Practice. Select the various kinds of ADF approach charts, as in the examples reproduced in Figs. 9-11 to 9-13. The simplest case is illustrated in Fig. 9-11, the NDB-A approach at Lakeview, Oreg. Here the NDB (GOOSE) is on the field. Choose some nearby NDB or broadcast station to simulate GOOSE. As in simulated VOR approaches, add or subtract an even number of thousands of feet to all altitudes shown on the chart, so that you can carry out the approach safely with respect to your actual terrain. Track inbound to the NDB as though you were making the transition from LAKEVIEW VOR; this means tracking inbound on a magnetic bearing of 148°, as shown. Then, maintaining the appropriate altitudes at each phase of the approach, track outbound on radial 161°, execute the procedure turn, and track inbound on magnetic bearing 341°, letting down to the MDA. Finally, execute the missed approach procedure as shown.

Fig. 9-12 illustrates an approach at Troutdale, Oreg. in which the NDB is collocated with an outer marker. Here the approach is inbound on the 061° bearing to LAKE, with stepwise letdowns (your check pilot will have to give you the simulated radar fixes). The final approach tracks the bearing of 061° from the NDB, with timing to the missed approach point. The missed approach will provide good practice in ADF holding at the NDB, in the pattern illustrated on the chart.

Finally, the NDB-A approach at Klamath Falls, Oreg. (Fig. 9-13) provides an exercise in ADF intersections as part of the transition to the approach. Begin on a heading of 162°, to the west of the approach course, as though you were transitioning from the LMT VOR. You have to identify MT DOME intersection, which is specified by a magnetic bearing of 027° to MERRILL NDB. At MT. DOME, you have to turn left and fly directly to the NDB, done most readily by the homing technique, since the distance is so short. Finally, at MERRILL, you'll turn left to intercept the 319° bearing from the NDB, and you'll track it inbound, as you let down on final approach. Since you won't have a marker beacon on your simulated approach, your check pilot will have to estimate it for you from the distances shown on the profile view. Then you'll time the final leg to the

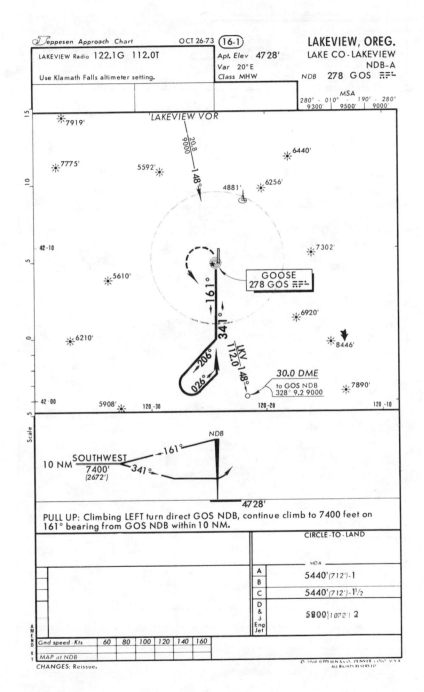

Fig. 9-11

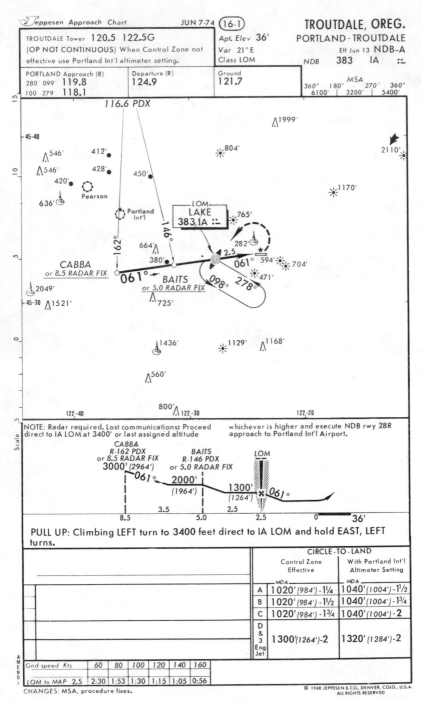

Fig. 9-12

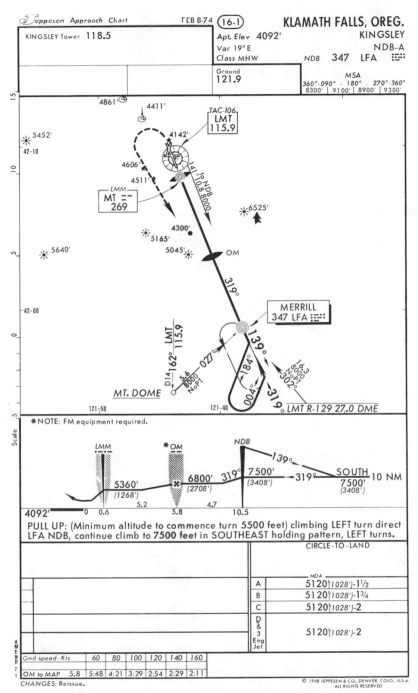

Fig. 9-13

missed approach point. The missed approach includes tracking inbound to the NDB, and then holding in the depicted pattern, after a parallel entry.

Scoring for these approaches and others like them follows exactly the same procedures as for VOR approaches.

Score Sheet: Simulated ADF Approaches.

Session:	1	2	3	4	5	6	7	8	9	10		
Date:												
ITEM												
Total number of simulated approaches.												
Airspeed deviation greater than 5 knots. (10 points)												
—— greater than 10 knots. (20 additional)												
Altitude deviation in level flight or level-off greater than 50 ft. (10 points)												
—— greater than 100 ft. (20 additional)												
Failure to repeat clearance. (10 points)												
Misinterpretation of approach plate. (50 points)												
Descent below minimums. (50 points)												
Exceeding allowed elapsed time, or failure to start timing, or miscalculation of time. (50 points)												
Sloppy initiation of missed approach. (20 points)												
TOTAL POINT SCORE												
FINAL SCORE (= Total Point Score divided by total number of simulated approaches.)												

10. ILS APPROACHES

Principles.

An ILS approach is a precision maneuver. Course guidance is provided by the localizer, to which your NAV needle is 4 times more sensitive than to ordinary VOR course guidance. Thus, full scale needle deflection corresponds to only 2.5 degrees off course. At the outer marker, typically 5 miles from touchdown, this represents about 1200 feet. At the middle marker, approximately one-half mile from touchdown (often the missed approach point), the distance from centerline to full needle deflection is only a few hundred feet. Glide slope guidance is provided by a beam that is directed upward from the runway at an angle of about 2.5 degrees. The glide path is very narrow in the vertical dimension—usually about 500 feet at the outer marker, about 200 feet at the middle marker.

As with most IFR procedures, the point is to have everything set up well in advance, so you can concentrate on flying the airplane during the final approach. Sometime during the transition from the enroute airway you should run through all your avionics equipment, setting each as appropriate. Set NAV #1 to the ILS frequency and identify the station. Set the OBS to the inbound course for ready reference, even though (unlike VOR) the OBS setting has no effect on the needle tuned to a localizer. Set NAV #2 as required for any intersection that has to be identified as part of the procedure, otherwise to a VOR that may be needed during a missed approach. Test the marker beacons and make sure the audio is on. Set up ADF and DME as required by the particular approach. Have your timing system (stopwatch or whatever) ready to be activated. One of your radios will be tuned already to approach control; set the other to the tower frequency. Then study the approach plate and become familiar with the essentials.

Each phase of an approach has its own particular essentials, upon which you'll want to concentrate. During the transition, outbound flight, and procedure turn, you'll want to be sure of the altitudes and times. Note especially that "Cleared for the approach" is not necessarily clearance to start a descent, but only says that you may proceed according to the charts. **If you haven't yet reached the fix at which the published transition begins, you must stay above the MEA or MOCA until that point is reached.** It is a good idea to time all segments of the procedure, starting with the transition. You want as much redundancy for backup as you can possibly get. Suppose you begin a transition from a VOR to intercept the localizer outbound, and the distance is given as 15.7 miles. Assuming your airspeed is 120 knots, you know that you must intercept the localizer in about 8 minutes. If the time passes and nothing happens to the needle, you'll be alerted at once to see what's wrong. Maybe a flag is showing, which you didn't notice before. Maybe you've inadvertently switched to a wrong frequency. Maybe the transmitter failed. It is impossible to over-emphasize how important timing becomes in situations like that. The alternative is increasing panic as you fly on into the unknown, without knowing just where you are, without even the assurance that you are in protected and safe airspace. Remember, also, that when you fly a LOC in the opposite direction to the normal inbound course, there is "reverse sensing", i.e., you correct back to centerline by flying away from the needle rather than toward it. Eventually, by timing or by reaching a specified fix, you will execute the procedure turn and return to intercept the LOC again to start the inbound phase of the procedure.

The remainder of a typical ILS procedure will be illustrated by Fig. 10-1, which is the ILS Rwy 30L approach at San Jose, Calif. Most ILS approaches are pretty much alike, and this one is fairly typical in all respects. Flying outbound on the LOC, your NAV #2 was set to 117.3 in order to identify LICK intersection, where you are permitted to begin your procedure turn. It is a good idea to fly outbound at least a full minute before starting the procedure turn, to ensure that regardless of the wind condition you will have plenty of time to get things settled down after you re-intercept turning inbound. Now, as you come out of your procedure turn, you intercept and center the LOC needle and proceed inbound. The plate shows two procedures: the full precision ILS procedure in solid lines on the profile, the nonprecision ILS procedure (i.e., without glide slope) in broken lines. For the ILS procedure, you start timing again at LICK, in order to estimate when you should intercept the glide slope, maintaining 4000' until then. From the mileages of the segments, you can see that from LICK to glide slope intercept is about 5 miles, i.e., about 2.5 minutes. It is important to intercept the glide slope properly because of the possibility of finding a "false glide slope" (a ghost radio beam or echo) and following it down.

As the glide slope needle centers, you make an immediate smooth power reduction and set up your approach speed and rate of descent, as described in Chapters 6 and 7. Your timer is still running, as a backup for arrival at the OM. DME (if you have it) provides yet another important backup throughout the whole ILS procedure. At the OM, the important thing to check is the altitude, since the altitude of the glide slope at the OM is always given on the approach plate. This is the guarantee (and the only one) that you are actually on the authentic glide slope. If you are not, a missed

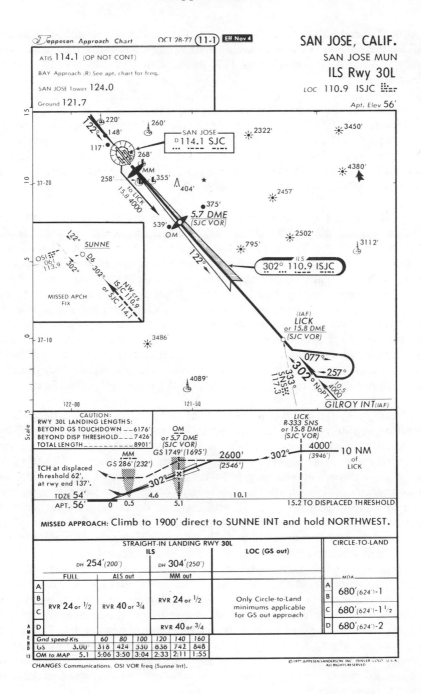

Fig. 10-1

approach is inevitable; go back and try again. This business about being on a false glide slope is not an exotic or imaginary hazard; it happens very easily and has happened to most IFR pilots, although they may not boast about it.

At the OM you do your final landing cockpit check, set up the approach configuration (GUMP = Gas, Undercarriage, Mixture, Prop; Fuelpump, etc.), report to the tower ("45 Juliet outer marker") and fly the airplane. Once your NAV #2 was no longer needed for LICK intersection, you should have switched it to 113.9 (OSI, 062°) in readiness for a missed approach and identified the station.

From the OM inbound there is nothing to do but fly the airplane. Staying exactly on course presents the same problems as with VOR approaches (Chapter 7), except that it is 4 times more difficult. You should try maintaining headings with rudder pressures and using very gentle aileron pressures to maintain wings level, to see if this technique may be best for you. You'll need pressure with both feet, a slight differential pressure giving you the best fine control. Alternatively you can combine slight aileron pressures with coordinated rudder pressures, or you can ignore the rudders and use only very gentle aileron movements. The whole point is to make tiny heading corrections very frequently, never letting the needle get more than the slightest bit off center. Exactly how you accomplish this doesn't matter; probably different people will find different techniques best.

Throughout the approach, your right hand is on the throttle, which controls the rate of descent. Some argue for staying on the glide slope by means of yoke movements, but this is very questionable. If you maintain the correct approach airspeed, one and only one power setting will keep you on the glide slope, and the only problem is to make small adjustments for local updrafts or downdrafts. If you are low on the glide slope, you do not have to actually pull up to it; all you have to do is reduce your rate of descent slightly and you will converge with it again—after all, the glide slope is going steadily downhill in front of you. Of course, you can reduce your rate of descent with elevator, but only at the expense of airspeed; and under some conditions only temporarily, followed by a faster rate of descent. In any case, in the long run, if the power setting isn't just right, you'll fly the whole approach at an average airspeed other than what you intended. Airspeed changes also affect elapsed time, which is an important backup for your missed approach point—another reason for flying an approach at constant airspeed. If it is agreed that constant airspeed is desirable, then the usual principle holds—the same principle you've learned and applied in your enroute flying—that yoke controls airspeed and throttle controls rate of descent.

The key to keeping the GS needle centered is the same as for the LOC needle—very small corrections made frequently. Avoid the temptation to overcorrect with large bursts of power and changes of pitch attitude. If you're a little high, reduce power a little, keep the airspeed constant, and wait. If what you just did doesn't stop the GS needle, but it continues to move, make another correction. Stopping the needle is the most important job. Then returning it to the center can be done in a more leisurely way.

The main problem you will find until you become experienced enough is that your scan will not be fast enough, and it will not be properly organized. Your eyes must keep moving, but not in a helter-skelter way. The key instrument, on which your eyes must be focused at least 90 percent of the time, is the AI. If you maintain wings exactly level, and if the ball is centered, you will hold a perfectly constant heading, all the way to touchdown. The correct manner of scanning is the "wagon-wheel" method. This means that the AI is the hub of a wheel, and all the other instruments are out on the spokes. Focus on the hub (the AI), then glance out at the DG to verify the correct heading, **then back to the AI**, then over to the needle to make sure it is well centered, **then back again to the AI**. A glance at the altimeter (keeping minimums in mind), **then back to the AI**. Check the airspeed, **then back to the AI**. Check the VSI, **then back to the AI**. And so it continues, all the way to minimums. If the needle tells you there is some wind drift, make an immediate correction of the heading with very slight bank or rudder pressure, then return again to the wings level condition **on the AI**.

All the while, you have two critical numbers to keep in mind—I prefer repeating them out loud—the decision height (DH) and the elapsed time to MAP. When your altitude approaches the DH, stop your descent briskly, by bringing in power, to avoid any possibility of descending below minimums. The hazards of sneaking a few feet lower to "have a look" have been pointed out already.

The missed approach procedure was discussed in Chapter 7, and you have already practiced it to perfection. The only thing at all different in ILS missed approaches is that one may be required to continue on the LOC course straight out during the climb. The LOC transmitter is at the far end of the runway. As you cross over it, there will be a momentary vacillation of the needle, which you should ignore. Then, as you fly out the other side, nothing changes. Don't make the mistake of thinking that you change to reverse sensing in that situation—you don't. As long as your direction of flight coincides with the inbound course, the sensing is the same, regardless of which side of the transmitter you're on.

Practice.

Unlike VOR approaches, which could be simulated with any VOR, the only way to practice ILS approaches is to fly real ones. If you are lucky enough to have a nearby ILS that isn't too busy, you can fly it again and again under the hood, with your check pilot keeping score. If it's a busy one, especially if there's a lot of jet traffic, try to pick a time of day when not much is going on. Otherwise you'll have two problems: First, the controller will constantly shunt you aside to bring in the jets, so it will take a long time to complete an approach. Second, there will always be the danger of wake turbulence. You'll have to request delays yourself, to place your airplane at least 2 minutes behind a commercial jet. And even then, you'll be wise to fly high on the glide slope—just decide to keep the glide slope needle in a definite low position rather than in the center. Fortunately, as with most complicated IFR procedures, much of your learning can be done on the ground. Fly imaginary ILS approaches in your own home, going through all the steps until they're second nature. You'll save airplane time and instructor time. Also, it is sensible not to practice ILS approaches at all until your VOR approaches are perfect and you are the complete master of the airplane in descents.

Scoring follows usual principles. It is tough, just as flying the ILS will be the toughest part of your check ride. Good luck!

Score Sheet

ITEM	1	2	3	4	5	6	7	8	9	10
Session:										
Date:										
Total number of approaches.										
Airspeed deviation greater than 5 knots. (10 points)										
—— greater than 10 knots. (20 additional)										
LOC needle off scale. (50 points)										
S-turns across the LOC course. (20 points)										
GS needle off scale. (50 points)										
Seesawing above and below GS. (20 points)										
Descent below DH. (50 points)										
Exceeding allowed elapsed time, or failure to start timing, or miscalculation of time. (50 points)										
Serious misinterpretation of approach plate. (50 points)										
Getting behind a rplane (failure to set things up in advance.) (20 points)										
Failure to repeat clearances or to report as required to ATC. (10 points)										
Sloppy missed approach procedure. (20 points)										
Failure to initiate missed approach procedure, resulting in potentially dangerous situation. (50 points)										
TOTAL POINT SCORE										
FINAL SCORE (= Total Point Score divided by total number of approaches.)